I0143611

Supervisor Success
Navigating the New
Leader Landscape

Dr. Patrick C. Patrong

President/CEO
Patrong Enterprises, Inc.

Richmond, VA

Supervisor Success: Navigating the New Leder Landscaper
© 2025 by Dr. Patrick C. Patrong

For information regarding permissions or speaking engagements, contact:
Patrong Enterprises, Inc.

Richmond, Virginia   Telephone/WhatsApp: 1.410.294.5431
Website: www.patrong.com   Email: info@patrong.com

All examples, case studies, and scenarios in this book are inspired by real organizational settings but are presented in a composite form to preserve confidentiality and learning value. Names, roles, and details have been altered.

Printed in the United States of America.

ISBN: 979-8-9998411-4-8

Library of Congress Control Number: *Pending*

Design and Layout: Patrong Enterprises, Inc. **Cover Design:** "PEI Creative Studio 1A

First Edition: 2025

Legal Disclaimer
This publication is intended to provide general leadership and supervisory guidance. It is not intended to substitute for legal, human resources, or compliance advice tailored to any specific organization. Readers should consult their agency or legal counsel before applying any policies or procedures discussed in this book.

DEDICATION

To the esteemed leaders and mentors who have guided me throughout my career, your wisdom, patience, and unwavering commitment to excellence have shaped the professional I am today. Each lesson you imparted, each challenge you helped me navigate, and each standard you set have been a cornerstone in my journey.

- Selwin Johnson, "Ten Days" Laborer
- Corporal Thomas, Drill Instructor, T&T Police Training College
- Sergeant Valley, T&T Police Guard and Emergency Branch
- Dr. Ruby Higgins, Grambling State University
- Dr. Earl Vincent, Grambling State University
- Valarie Long, Service Employees International Union
- Walter Ginn, Baltimore City Department of Social Services
- Gloria Valentine, Maryland Department of Social Services
- Karen Moody, Esq. Baltimore City Human Resources
- Dr. Elliott Wheelan, Baltimore/Richmond City Human Resources
- Valary Rawlings, University of Phoenix
- Nancy Flannagan, Virginia Department of Social Services
- Donna Douglas, Virginia Department of Social Services
- Marjorie Powell, University of Maryland, Baltimore
- Susan Mongold, Virginia Department of Emergency Management
- Dr. Jameo Pollock, Virginia Department of Transportation
- Kimberly Wilson, Virginia Museum of Fine Arts
- Caprice Bragg, Virginia Museum of Fine Arts

Your leadership was more than instruction; it was an example of resilience, integrity, and influence. May your legacies continue to inspire those who follow, as you inspired me.

ACKNOWLEDGMENTS

To those who have entrusted me with the privilege of leadership and those who have allowed me to learn under their guidance, I extend my deepest gratitude. Leadership is a shared experience—one that flourishes through trust, challenge, and collaboration.

To my former supervisors, thank you for your patience, insight, and belief in my potential. Your guidance sharpened my skills, strengthened my character, and instilled in me the responsibility of leading with purpose. You provided the framework upon which I built my own leadership philosophy, and for that, I am eternally grateful.

To my colleagues, direct reports, and fellow professionals, you have been integral to my journey, offering perspectives that deepened my understanding of leadership and service. Together, we have created environments that foster growth, innovation, and impact.

To the mentors who set the standard and the followers who placed their trust in me—your influence is woven into my professional journey. The lessons learned, the challenges overcome, and the successes achieved are a testament to the power of shared leadership.

This acknowledgment is dedicated to those who have been part of my path, whether through guidance, partnership, or shared purpose. Our collective efforts have made a difference, and together, we will continue to inspire change.

CONTENTS

No table of contents entries found.

PREFACE

Stepping into supervision is both an honor and a challenge. For more than three decades, I have witnessed the unique struggles and triumphs of those called to lead others. Too often, supervisors are promoted because of technical expertise rather than leadership readiness. The result is a silent tension: new leaders feel unprepared, employees feel uncertain, and organizations miss opportunities to thrive.

This book was born out of the conviction that supervision does not have to be overwhelming. With the right guidance, supervisors can transform their roles from sources of stress into platforms of growth — for themselves, their teams, and their organizations. My journey through public service, higher education, and cultural institutions has shown me that effective supervision is not about titles or authority; it is about influence, character, and consistency.

What you will find in these chapters is not theory alone but tested strategies, real-world case examples, and practical tools. The concepts are drawn from my experiences coaching leaders at every level, teaching across diverse organizations, and learning through my own successes and mistakes. They are presented here to equip you with clarity, confidence, and actionable steps for your supervisory journey.

This book is also deeply personal. My philosophy of leadership has been shaped by mentors, colleagues, and those who entrusted me with responsibility long before I felt ready. It has been refined by mistakes that humbled me and by moments of breakthrough when I saw people grow because of encouragement and accountability. These pages carry the lessons of that journey, distilled for your use.

As you read, I encourage you to pause at the reflection questions, adapt the tools to your context, and treat supervision not as a burden but as a privilege. Leadership is not about perfection; it is about persistence — showing up each day with integrity, empathy, and courage.

May these pages serve as a companion, a coach, and a catalyst as you chart your own path of supervisory success.

—Dr. Patrick C. Patrong

1 THRIVING AMIDST CHALLENGES
The Journey of New Supervisors

Introduction – A New Chapter, A New Challenge

The day you are promoted to supervisor is a proud moment. It comes with a new title, a new desk, and a new authority. But it also comes with a silent weight — a responsibility that is often underestimated until you feel it pressing on your shoulders.

One supervisor I coached recently told me, *"I thought being promoted meant I finally had control. Instead, I felt like I was being pulled in every direction — my team wanted answers, my boss wanted results, and I wasn't sure where to start."*

If that sounds familiar, you're not alone. New supervisors quickly learn that success requires more than technical skill. It requires adaptability, people skills, and the ability to balance expectations from above and below. This chapter is designed to help you step confidently into that challenge, embrace the reality of supervision, and set the tone for your leadership journey.

Section 1 – Understanding the Challenge

Supervisors occupy one of the most challenging spaces in an organization — the middle. They receive pressure from leadership to deliver results, while also serving as the frontline support for employees. Research shows that nearly 60% of new supervisors receive little or no training before stepping into the role, which explains why many feel overwhelmed in their first year.

The most common challenges include:

- Dual identity: Yesterday, you were a peer; today, you are a leader.

- Unclear expectations: Promotions often happen because of technical expertise, not leadership readiness.

- Balancing people and process: Supervisors must manage workflow and build trust at the same time.

- Pressure cooker environment: You are accountable to employees and senior leaders.

Understanding these dynamics upfront allows you to prepare. You are not just learning to manage tasks — you are learning to navigate the complexities of human interactions.

Section 2 – Shifting from Individual Contributor to Leader

Perhaps the most significant adjustment is recognizing that your value no longer lies in what you personally produce, but in what your team accomplishes. This is the leadership identity shift.

I describe it as The Three Critical Shifts every supervisor must make:

1. From Doing → Enabling: Your job is to clear roadblocks so others can succeed.

2. From Me → We: Team results are now the measure of your success.

3. From Control → Influence: Real authority is built on trust, not position.

Magic with a Message: I often perform a rope illusion called *The Professor's Nightmare.* Three ropes of different lengths suddenly become equal. The lesson is simple: people may come to you with different experiences. Still, the role of the supervisor is to create alignment, so every team member feels empowered to contribute equally.

Section 3 – Overcoming Misconceptions

New supervisors often stumble because of unrealistic expectations. Let's tackle the most common ones:

- "I must have all the answers."
  Reality: Great supervisors ask great questions and seek input before deciding.

- "I should be everyone's friend."
  Reality: Leadership is built on respect, not popularity. Being too focused on friendships can erode accountability.

- "Discipline makes me the bad guy."
  Reality: Fair and consistent standards build trust and safety. Employees want to know the rules are applied equally.

- "If I work harder, my team will follow."
  Reality: Burnout is not a leadership strategy. Model balance and efficiency instead.

To illustrate: a supervisor I once observed tried to avoid conflict by overlooking small policy violations. At first, employees loved him for it. But within six months, productivity dropped, and team tension increased. Why? The absence of accountability created confusion. Respect was lost.

Section 4 – Growing Personally and Professionally

Supervision is not just a professional shift — it is a personal growth journey. Every new supervisor must learn about their own blind spots, triggers, and strengths.

Consider these Four Lenses of Growth:

1. Skill – Do I have the technical and managerial skills I need?

2. Character – Do I fairly demonstrate integrity and consistency?

3. Emotional Intelligence – Do I understand and regulate my emotions while reading others?

4. Resilience – Can I recover quickly when setbacks come?

Supervisors who actively cultivate these four areas position themselves to thrive not only in their current role but also in future leadership opportunities.

Public Sector Case Snapshot

Angela, a newly promoted supervisor in a government office, inherited a discouraged team. Her predecessor had focused only on output, neglecting recognition and employee development. Angela decided to take a different approach.

In her first month, she scheduled one-on-one conversations with each employee. She didn't bring a checklist of directives. Instead, she asked three questions:

1. What do you enjoy most about your job?

2. What obstacles make your work harder?

3. What is one improvement you'd like to see?

By month three, the team had implemented two of the suggested changes, morale was noticeably higher, and absenteeism dropped. Angela's success was not about flashy initiatives. It was about listening, valuing input, and acting on it.

Applied Tool – Supervisor's First 90 Days Roadmap

The first 90 days of supervision often define how your team perceives you. Use this roadmap as a guide:

Days 1–30: Listen and Learn

- Meet with each employee individually.
- Ask questions, don't prescribe solutions.
- Clarify expectations with your own supervisor.

Days 31–60: Build Momentum

- Identify and deliver small wins that matter to the team.
- Begin introducing team goals collaboratively.
- Communicate progress regularly.

Days 61–90: Establish Leadership

- Set clear performance standards.
- Delegate responsibilities with accountability.
- Create your own development plan as a supervisor.

Supervisors who follow this pattern send a clear message: *I value people, I set direction, and I am committed to growth.*

Reflection Questions

1. What excites me most about being a supervisor? What concerns me most?

2. Which of the Three Critical Shifts (Doing → Enabling, Me → We, Control → Influence) will be hardest for me? Why?

3. Which misconception about supervision have I believed in the past? How can I challenge it?

4. What specific action will I take in my first week to show my leadership style?

5. How can I model resilience for my team when they experience challenges moment, situations, and people?

Leadership-Centered Summary

Supervision is a privilege and a test. You are now responsible not only for results but also for people. Thriving in this new role requires embracing the challenges, shifting your identity, letting go of misconceptions, and committing to continuous personal growth.

You don't have to be perfect. You simply have to be intentional. When you start with listening, build credibility through small wins, and model the leadership behaviors you expect from others, you will establish a foundation for long-term success.

"Supervisory success is not measured by how much you accomplish alone, but by how much growth you inspire in those you lead."

- Dr. Patrick C. Patrong.

"The true measure of a supervisor is not how they handle the easy days, but how they inspire growth in themselves and their team in the midst of challenges."

- Dr. Patrick C. Patrong.

2 NAVIGATING CHANGE
A Supervisor's Odyssey in a Shifting World

Introduction – The Only Constant is Change

If there is one truth every supervisor must embrace, it is this: change is inevitable. New policies, shifting priorities, technological upgrades, budget adjustments, and organizational restructuring are part of today's workplace reality. For supervisors, change brings opportunity and uncertainty.

One supervisor once told me, "Every time we get comfortable, the rules change again. My team looks to me for stability, but I don't always feel steady myself." That tension captures the supervisor's challenge — to be a steady presence even in the midst of turbulence.

In this chapter, we will explore what it means to lead through change, not simply react to it. You will see that successful supervisors don't resist change or rush blindly into it. They learn how to navigate it, guide their people through it, and emerge stronger on the other side.

Section 1 – Understanding the Dynamics of Change

Change is rarely just about a new system or process. It is about people — their fears, their habits, and their sense of security. Supervisors must recognize:

- Change disrupts comfort zones. Employees may resist not because they dislike progress, but because they fear losing competence.

- Change creates uncertainty. The unknown often triggers anxiety that must be addressed.

- Change tests trust. If employees trust leadership, they will embrace the journey. If they don't, even small changes can create turmoil.

- Supervisors who anticipate these dynamics are better prepared to lead effectively.

Section 2 – The Supervisor's Role in Leading Through Change

While senior leadership may set the direction, it is supervisors who make change real for employees. Your role is to:

- Communicate clearly and consistently. Silence breeds rumors.

- Translate vision into practice. Employees need to know how the change affects their daily work.

- Model adaptability. If you panic, your team will panic. If you remain steady, they will feel steadier.

- Support employees. Listening to concerns and offering reassurance creates trust.

Remember: supervisors are the bridge between strategy and execution. Without you, change stalls.

Section 3 – Strategies for Embracing and Driving Change

Here are four practical strategies supervisors can use:

1. Acknowledge the Disruption. Pretending nothing has changed undermines credibility. Name the shift honestly.

2. Create Quick Wins. Find early, small successes to show progress and build momentum.

3. Involve Your Team. Invite input on how to adapt processes. Ownership reduces resistance.

4. Keep the Big Picture Visible. Employees need to understand not just the "what," but the "why" behind the change.

Magic with a Message: One of my favorite illusions involves pouring water into a newspaper, crumpling it, and then opening it to reveal the pages completely dry. The message: things might seem chaotic on the surface, but with the proper preparation, you can stay steady through uncertainty. Supervisors bring that stability to their teams during times of change.

Section 4 – The Growth Opportunity in Change

Change is not simply an obstacle — it is a chance to grow as a leader. Every shift provides supervisors with the opportunity to:

- Build credibility through calm, confident leadership.

- Strengthen relationships with employees by showing empathy.

- Develop new skills in problem-solving, innovation, and resilience.

Supervisors who view change as an opportunity instead of a threat find themselves not just surviving transitions but positioning themselves for advancement.

Public Sector Case Snapshot

When the Department of Transportation implemented a new digital timekeeping system, many employees resisted. They felt the old paper system was simpler. John, a frontline supervisor, decided to take a proactive approach.

Instead of simply announcing the change, he scheduled a demo with his team and personally walked them through the system. He acknowledged their frustration but highlighted the benefits — reduced errors, faster approvals, and more flexibility. Within weeks, his team had one of the smoothest adoptions in the agency.

The difference was not the system. It was John's approach: acknowledging resistance, guiding patiently, and modeling confidence.

Applied Tool – The Supervisor's Change Leadership Checklist
Use this checklist when guiding your team through any organizational change:

Before Change is Announced:

- Gather facts — understand the "what" and "why."

- Anticipate employee concerns.

- Prepare your own talking points.

During Implementation:

- Communicate frequently and consistently.

- Hold short team huddles to share updates.

- Address resistance directly and respectfully.

- Celebrate small wins and early adopters.

After Change is in Place:

- Evaluate what went well and what didn't.

- Solicit team feedback on the process.

- Recognize those who adapted quickly.

- Document lessons learned for next time.

Reflection Questions

1. How do I typically respond to change — with excitement, hesitation, or resistance?

2. What fears or concerns might my team experience during change?

3. How can I communicate more clearly when changes occur?

4. What is one "quick win" I can deliver to help my team adapt faster?

5. How can I use change as a personal growth opportunity instead of just a challenge?

Leadership-Centered Summary

Change is not optional. But how you lead through it is. As a supervisor, you are the steady hand guiding your team through uncertainty. By anticipating fears, communicating clearly, and modeling adaptability, you can transform resistance into momentum.

The best supervisors do more than survive change — they use it as a stage to demonstrate leadership.

"Change will always test you, but it also gives you the chance to show your team the kind of leader you really are."
- Dr. Patrick C. Patrong

3 FROM NOVICE TO NAVIGATOR
Essential Survival Skills for New Leaders

Introduction – Finding Your Bearings

Every supervisor begins their journey in the same place: uncertainty. Even the most confident employees discover that stepping into a leadership role changes everything. You no longer measure success by your individual output; your effectiveness now depends on how you influence, guide, and inspire others.

I once worked with a supervisor who described their promotion as the proudest and scariest day of their career. They said, "I knew how to be the best at my job. What I didn't know was how to help others be their best." That moment captures the reality of supervision. You are not expected to have all the answers immediately. You are expected to grow into the role.

This chapter equips you with the survival skills you need during those early months. Think of these as your compass, anchor, and navigation chart — the essentials that transform you from a novice into a leader capable of steering a team through uncharted waters.

Section 1 – Core Traits of Effective Supervisors

The first survival skill is cultivating the traits that make supervisors credible in the eyes of their teams.

Effective supervisors are:

- **Consistent** – Employees must know what to expect from you. If you praise one day and criticize the next for the same behavior, your team will become uncertain and disengaged.

- **Fair** – Fairness is about more than rules. It is about applying standards evenly and showing no favoritism.

- **Communicative** – Silence breeds suspicion. Communicate openly, even when you do not have all the answers.

None of these traits are innate. They are daily practices. Consistency requires you to pause before reacting so you do not contradict yourself. Fairness requires you to set aside personal preferences and look at issues objectively. Communication requires you to choose clarity over comfort, even when the truth may be difficult to share.

These traits form the bedrock of trust. Without trust, no skill, strategy, or tool will make you effective.

Section 2 – Building Self-Awareness

The second survival skill is self-awareness. Leadership begins with knowing yourself. Self-awareness means recognizing your leadership style, emotional triggers, and blind spots. Some supervisors are naturally directive, while others are collaborative. Neither style is wrong, but being unaware of your tendencies can cause you to overuse one approach when another is needed.

Emotional triggers can also derail new supervisors. For example, if you struggle with criticism, you may overreact to employee complaints. If you crave approval, you may avoid holding employees accountable. Identifying these triggers helps you respond thoughtfully instead of impulsively.

Practical ways to build self-awareness include keeping a leadership journal, seeking feedback from peers and mentors, and reflecting on tough situations to identify what worked and what did not. Supervisors who commit to this practice become more resilient and more authentic in their leadership.

Section 3 – Decision-Making and Problem-Solving

The third survival skill is decision-making. Leadership requires you to make choices under pressure.

Indecision can paralyze a team. Employees look to their supervisors for direction. When leaders hesitate too long, frustration builds. The key is not to rush blindly but to gather enough information to act with confidence.

Effective decision-making involves:
- Gathering input from employees closest to the issue.
- Analyzing facts without becoming stuck in endless research.
- Making a choice, then monitoring outcomes and adjusting if necessary.

Remember: no decision will ever have perfect information. Progress is more important than perfection. As one seasoned supervisor put it, "I'd rather make a decision that needs tweaking than no decision at all."

Section 4 – Emotional Intelligence and Interpersonal Skills

The fourth survival skill is emotional intelligence (EQ). EQ is the ability to recognize, understand, and manage emotions in yourself and others.

Supervisors with high EQ notice when tensions rise before they escalate into conflict. They listen beyond words, paying attention to tone and body language. They know when to push employees and when to offer support.

Developing EQ involves practicing active listening, asking clarifying questions, and regulating your own emotions before addressing others. For example, if an employee's mistake frustrates you, pause before responding. Address the issue calmly and constructively. Employees will respect your fairness and composure, even when receiving corrective feedback.

Interpersonal skills also extend to building relationships. A supervisor who invests in knowing their employees' strengths, challenges, and aspirations will be more effective in motivating them.

Public Sector Case Snapshot

Carla, a new supervisor in a county office, inherited a team of veteran employees. Many were skeptical of her leadership because she was younger and less experienced. They expected her to enforce rules rigidly to prove authority.

Instead, Carla took a different path. She began by meeting with each employee individually. She asked about their experiences, listened to their frustrations, and acknowledged their expertise. By demonstrating humility and consistency, she gradually earned their trust.

Six months later, the same employees who doubted her were volunteering to pilot new initiatives. Carla did not win them over with authority alone. She won them over with self-awareness, emotional intelligence, and respect.

Applied Tool – The Supervisor's Survival Kit

To thrive as a new supervisor, keep this survival kit at hand:

- **Patience** – Recognize that building credibility takes time.
- **Humility** – Be willing to admit what you do not know and seek guidance.
- **Communication** – Keep information flowing, even when it is incomplete.
- **Boundaries** – Protect your focus by setting limits on distractions.
- **Reflection** – Evaluate your performance weekly and identify lessons learned.

Tip: Use a journal or digital planner to track situations that challenged you, how you responded, and how you might improve next time. Over time, this becomes a powerful record of growth.

Reflection Questions

1. Which core trait of effective supervision (consistency, fairness, communication) is my strongest? Which needs the most development?

2. What personal triggers tend to influence my leadership style, and how can I manage them better?

3. How do I make decisions under pressure — do I lean toward overanalyzing or rushing?

4. In what ways am I practicing emotional intelligence on my team?

5. What steps can I take in the next 30 days to strengthen my supervisor survival skills?

Leadership-Centered Summary

The first months of supervision are exhilarating and intimidating. You may feel like a novice, but by cultivating the right survival skills, you can quickly begin navigating with confidence.

Core traits, such as consistency, fairness, and effective communication, lay the foundation. Self-awareness strengthens your leadership identity. Decision-making builds trust. Emotional intelligence fosters connection. Together, these skills transform uncertainty into influence.

Remember: no supervisor begins fully prepared. Leadership is a journey of growth. With practice and reflection, you will not only survive the early storms of supervision — you will emerge as a navigator capable of guiding your team to success.

"The best navigators are not those who avoid storms, but those who learn how to sail through them."

— Dr. Patrick C. Patrong.

4 UNLEASH YOUR LEADERSHIP POTENTIAL
The Art of Supervisory Mastery

Introduction – From Competence to Mastery

Many supervisors stop at competence. They learn the rules, meet expectations, and manage tasks. Competence keeps the organization afloat, but it does not inspire people or create change.

Mastery, on the other hand, is the art of transforming supervision into leadership. It is about creating trust, shaping culture, and empowering people to excel. Competence is about *what you do*. Mastery is about *who you are as a leader*.

I once met a supervisor in a public health department who described their transition this way: "At first, I thought being a supervisor was about proving I knew everything. Later, I realized it was about helping my team shine. That shift changed everything."

This chapter will guide you through the journey from competence to mastery, equipping you with the mindset, tools, and practices to unleash your leadership potential.

Section 1 – Defining Supervisory Leadership

Supervisory leadership goes beyond assigning tasks and enforcing rules. It is the ability to inspire others while ensuring accountability. At its core, supervisory leadership involves three functions:

- **Direction** – Providing clarity on goals and priorities.

- **Support** – Equipping employees with the resources, coaching, and encouragement they need.

- **Accountability** – Holding employees responsible for results fairly and consistently.

Many new supervisors struggle to balance these functions. They may emphasize accountability but neglect support, or offer support without clear direction. Mastery means integrating all three.

A supervisor who embodies leadership understands that employees are not just workers; they are people with strengths, aspirations, and challenges. Supervisory leadership means recognizing the human side of management.

Section 2 – Developing a Leadership Philosophy

Great supervisors are guided by a personal leadership philosophy — a set of beliefs and values that shape decisions and actions. Without one, leadership becomes reactive and inconsistent.

To develop your philosophy, reflect on questions such as:

- What do I believe about people?

- What values will I never compromise?

- What's a supervisor's role in employee development?

- How do I define fairness?

Your philosophy does not need to be complex. It might be as simple as: "I believe people do their best when they feel valued. My role is to create an environment where they can succeed.

Once defined, your philosophy becomes your compass. It ensures that even in difficult situations, you lead with consistency and integrity. Employees notice when supervisors act from a place of principle.

Section 3 – Learning from Exemplary Leaders

One of the fastest ways to grow as a leader is to observe others. Exemplary supervisors often share common practices:

- They remain calm under pressure.

- They communicate clearly and consistently.

- They give credit generously and accept responsibility when things go wrong.

- They invest in the growth of their employees.

Take time to identify leaders you admire. Study how they interact with their teams, how they handle crises, and how they make decisions. Ask yourself: *What can I model from their example? What lessons can I adapt to my own leadership?*

Remember, mastery is not imitation. It is about learning from others while staying authentic to your own values and style.

Section 4 – The Path to Mastery

Mastery does not happen overnight. It is the result of deliberate practice, feedback, and reflection. Think of it as a four-step process:

1. **Learn** – Gain knowledge through training, mentoring, and study.

2. **Apply** – Put knowledge into practice with your team.

3. **Reflect** – Analyze what worked, what did not, and why.

4. **Refine** – Adjust your approach and improve with each cycle.

This process is continuous. Just as athletes train daily to refine their skills, supervisors must continually practice leadership behaviors. Each challenge is an opportunity to sharpen your craft.

Supervisory mastery is less about reaching a destination and more about embracing leadership as a lifelong journey.

Public Sector Case Snapshot

Derrick, a supervisor in a state corrections facility, quickly discovered that authority alone was not enough. Initially, he enforced rules strictly, believing that firmness equaled respect. Instead, he faced resistance and low morale.

After attending a leadership workshop, Derrick began developing his own leadership philosophy, rooted in fairness and transparency. He started holding regular team meetings where he invited input. He explained the reasons behind policies rather than just issuing directives.

Within a year, staff turnover decreased significantly, and incidents of conflict within his unit dropped. Derrick's shift from authority-driven supervision to principle-driven leadership demonstrated the power of mastery.

Applied Tool – Leadership Philosophy Builder

Use this tool to clarify and document your leadership philosophy.

- Step 1: Define Your Beliefs About People.
  - Do you believe employees want to succeed? Do you believe growth happens through coaching? Write your assumptions.
- Step 2: Identify Your Core Values
  - List three values that guide your leadership (e.g., integrity, fairness, respect).
- Step 3: State Your Role as a Supervisor
  - How do you see your responsibility to your team? To the organization?

- Step 4: Write Your Leadership Statement
  - o Combine your beliefs, values, and role into a few sentences. For example: "I believe employees thrive when they feel supported and challenged. My role is to set clear expectations, provide resources, and model fairness."

Revisit this statement regularly. Adjust it as your leadership grows.

Reflection Questions

1. How do I currently define my role as a supervisor?

2. What values influence my decisions at work?

3. Which leaders do I admire, and what qualities do they exhibit?

4. How can I begin to develop my own leadership philosophy?

5. What deliberate practices will I commit to that move me from competence toward mastery?

6. Are my team and I growing in mastery of leadership skills?

7. In what areas do I rely on authority rather than influence?

Leadership-Centered Summary

Supervisory mastery is about more than managing tasks — it is about unleashing your leadership potential. By defining a leadership philosophy, learning from others, and practicing deliberately, you elevate from competence to influence.

Your employees are watching not only what you do but how you do it. Mastery means leading with consistency, principle, and vision. It means moving from being a manager of work to being a leader of people. Competence may keep the ship afloat. Mastery sets the course.

"Competence keeps the ship afloat; mastery sets the course for the journey."
— Dr. Patrick C. Patrong

5 TIME
Your Most Precious Resource

Introduction – The Supervisor's Balancing Act

Every supervisor receives the same deposit of time each morning: 24 hours. What separates effective leaders from overwhelmed ones is not how much time they have, but how intentionally they use it.

Consider two supervisors in the same department. Both arrive at 8:00 a.m. with full calendars. One spends the day putting out fires, bouncing from email to phone calls to drop-in conversations. By 5:00 p.m., they are exhausted, frustrated, and unsure of what they actually accomplished. The other begins with a plan, protects blocks of time for critical work, and empowers employees to handle routine issues. By the end of the day, they feel tired but satisfied, with progress made on meaningful goals.

Both had the same number of hours. The difference was not in effort but in mastery of time. As a supervisor, how you manage time shapes not only your own effectiveness but also the culture and productivity of your entire team.

Section 1 – Understanding the Value of Time

Time is the most precious — and most limited — resource supervisors have. Unlike money, time cannot be borrowed, saved, or reclaimed once it is gone. The way you manage it signals your priorities, your values, and your leadership style.

Studies show that frontline supervisors lose **two to three hours per day** to interruptions, distractions, and unplanned requests. Over the course of a year, that equals more than **700 hours** — the equivalent of nearly 90 workdays. The cost of lost time is not just in productivity but also in decision fatigue, burnout, and strained employee relationships.

Think of time as currency. Each meeting, task, or email is a transaction. The question is: are you investing your time for the greatest return, or spending it carelessly? Supervisors who fail to value their time inevitably find themselves stretched thin and unable to focus on what matters most.

Section 2 – The Supervisor's Time Pyramid

To manage time effectively, supervisors must operate with a clear structure. Imagine a pyramid with three layers:

- **Foundation** – Routine Management: Handling tasks, scheduling, approving requests. These are necessary but should not consume all your time.

- **Middle** – Team Development: Coaching, feedback, and training. This is where supervisors build capacity and reduce future time drains.

- **Top** – Strategic Leadership: Planning, innovation, and improvement. Time at the top drives long-term success.

- **Capstone – Self-Reflection and Renewal:** Reviewing your own performance, maintaining work-life balance, and ensuring continuous personal growth. Supervisors who invest time here sustain clarity, resilience, and long-term effectiveness.

Too many supervisors spend nearly all their time at the base of the pyramid, reacting to daily demands. Mastery requires deliberately shifting upward, investing energy in developing people and leading strategically.

A useful reflection is: *Am I spending my time where it adds the most value, or am I stuck at the bottom of the pyramid?*

Section 3 – Principles of Time Management

There are three timeless principles every supervisor should master: **Plan, Prioritize, Protect.**

Plan – Begin each week with clarity about what matters most. Identify outcomes, not just tasks. A plan provides direction and reduces wasted effort.

Prioritize – Learn to distinguish between urgent and important. Urgent demands scream the loudest, but important tasks build long-term value. The Eisenhower Matrix is an excellent tool for sorting tasks.

Protect – Guard your focus. If you don't set boundaries, others will. Protecting time means limiting interruptions, delegating wisely, and saying no when necessary.

The Three Time Traps

Supervisors often fall into predictable traps:

1. **The Firefighter Trap:** Spending every day putting out emergencies without addressing root causes.

2. **The Perfectionist Trap:** Spending excessive time polishing tasks that are already good enough.

3. **The People-Pleaser Trap:** Saying yes to every request and spreading yourself too thin.

Awareness of these traps allows you to step back and make intentional choices about your time.

Section 4 – Setting Priorities and Boundaries

Prioritization is not about doing more; it is about doing what matters most. Supervisors who fail to prioritize end up reactive, overwhelmed, and ineffective.

The Eisenhower Matrix can help:

- Urgent and Important: Act immediately.

- Important but Not Urgent: Schedule and plan.

- Urgent but Not Important: Delegate.

- Neither Urgent nor Important: Eliminate.

Boundaries are equally important. Without them, supervisors risk becoming available 24/7. Boundaries might mean:

- Setting specific hours for open-door availability

- Establishing "focus blocks" on your calendar.

- Limiting after-hours emails.

Here is a respectful script for setting a boundary:

"I appreciate you bringing this up. Right now I need to focus on [priority task]. Let's set a time later today to discuss it, or is there someone else who could help in the meantime?"

By modeling boundaries, you give your employees permission to set their own, creating a healthier work environment.

Section 5 – Leveraging Technology Wisely

Technology can either be a supervisor's best ally or greatest distraction. Used well, it streamlines tasks and improves communication. Used poorly, it creates constant interruptions.

Helpful practices include:

- Using calendars and project tools to reduce redundant meetings.

- Automating reminders and routine updates.

- Creating "notification rules" so only urgent alerts interrupt you.

Harmful practices include:

- Checking email constantly instead of at scheduled times.

- Letting group chats dominate your attention.

- Relying on too many platforms, creating confusion.

Case Example: In one agency, meetings consumed nearly half of every supervisor's week. By adopting a shared project management tool, teams moved updates online. Meetings were reduced by 40%, freeing supervisors for coaching and planning. The lesson: technology should serve you, not control you.

Public Sector Case Snapshot

Maria, a municipal supervisor, was drowning in interruptions. Employees stopped by her office constantly with questions. Other departments called her directly with requests. She felt she never had time for the work that mattered most.

Through coaching, Maria adopted three changes:

- She blocked two hours each morning for uninterrupted focus, turning off email and phone alerts.

- She introduced a weekly huddle where employees could raise routine issues, reducing constant interruptions.

- She delegated administrative tasks to a senior staff member eager for more responsibility.

- She reorganized her calendar to group similar tasks together, reducing the time lost to switching between different types of work.

- She set clear expectations with other departments about preferred times and methods for communication, which cut down on last-minute requests and phone calls.

The change was dramatic. Maria reported lower stress, greater productivity, and better morale in her team. Employees appreciated her focus and clarity, and the delegated employee flourished in their expanded role.

Maria's story illustrates that time mastery is not about squeezing more tasks into a day. It is about creating systems that protect focus and empower others.

Applied Tool – The Supervisor's Time Mastery Planner

Supervisors need a daily and weekly system to manage time.

Weekly Planner

- Monday: Identify three outcomes for the week.

- Tuesday: Block time for high-priority projects.

- Wednesday: Reassess and adjust priorities.

- Thursday: Block time for high-priority projects.

- Friday: Reflect on progress and lessons learned.

Daily Focus Template

1. Top three priorities for today.

2. Delegated tasks.

3. Quick wins (tasks under 15 minutes).

4. Boundaries (when you will limit email, when you will end work).

5. Reflection: Did I use my time as intended today?

Using this planner helps supervisors design their days with intention instead of drifting into reactivity.

Reflection Questions

1. Where am I currently losing the most time each week?

2. Which of the Three Time Traps do I often fall into, and why?

3. How can I apply the Eisenhower Matrix to my current workload?

4. What boundaries do I need to establish to protect my focus?

5. How can I model healthy time practices for my team?

6. What task can I delegate to create more time for strategic work?

7. How can I use technology to reduce distractions instead of increasing them?

Leadership-Centered Summary

Time is the supervisor's most precious resource. Managing it well requires intention, discipline, and courage. Supervisors who plan, prioritize, and protect their time not only accomplish more but also model balance for their teams.

Your time choices communicate your leadership. When you prioritize development, you signal that people matter. When you protect focus, you demonstrate discipline. When you model boundaries, you create a culture of respect.

Remember: supervisors do not just manage tasks — they manage time, and in doing so, they set the pace for the entire team.

"Supervisors don't manage time; they manage themselves in relation to time — and in doing so, they set the pace for their teams."

— Dr. Patrick C. Patrong

6 PRODUCTIVITY UNLEASHED
Orchestrating the Work of Many

Introduction – Beyond Busyness

One of the most common mistakes supervisors make is equating busyness with productivity. A workplace full of ringing phones, constant meetings, and employees rushing from task to task may look productive, but the appearance of motion does not guarantee meaningful results. True productivity is not about working harder or longer — it is about working smarter, with focus and coordination.

I once observed two supervisors in the same department. Both had highly skilled employees and similar workloads. The first supervisor operated in constant crisis mode. Every issue came across their desk, and every decision required their approval. The team worked hard, but morale was low and mistakes were frequent. The second supervisor took a different approach. They delegated tasks based on strengths, clarified priorities, and empowered employees to solve problems. The result was a calm, focused team that consistently exceeded expectations.

The difference was orchestration. Like a conductor leading an orchestra, the supervisor's job is not to play every instrument but to ensure that each musician knows their role and contributes to a unified performance. Productivity is not achieved by adding more notes but by ensuring the right notes are played at the right time.

Section 1 – Redefining Productivity

To unleash productivity, supervisors must first redefine it. Productivity is not about activity — it is about outcomes. A team that produces ten reports filled with errors is less productive than a team that produces five accurate, impactful reports.

True productivity is measured by:

- Achievement of meaningful results.

- Efficiency in processes without sacrificing quality.

- Sustainability of effort over time — avoiding burnout.

- Alignment with organizational goals and mission.

When supervisors emphasize activity over outcomes, they risk rewarding inefficiency. Redefining productivity requires supervisors to set clear expectations, measure results, and encourage employees to focus on what matters most rather than simply staying busy.

Section 2 – Systems Thinking and Process Improvement

Every team functions within systems — the patterns and processes that govern how work is accomplished. Inefficient systems drain productivity, no matter how dedicated employees are. Supervisors must therefore learn to think in terms of systems and processes, not individual tasks.

Questions to ask include:

- Are steps being duplicated unnecessarily?

- Where are the bottlenecks that slow progress?

- Can routine tasks be automated or streamlined?

- Are handoffs between departments smooth or clumsy?

For example, in one public agency, employees were required to enter identical information into three different databases. The process wasted hours of staff time each week. By working with IT to integrate systems, the supervisor reduced duplication, cut processing time nearly in half, and freed employees to focus on higher-value work.

Improving systems often yields bigger gains than pushing employees to work harder. Supervisors who invest in process improvement set their teams up for sustained productivity.

Section 3 – The Power of Delegation

Delegation is one of the most underused tools of productivity. Many supervisors avoid delegation out of fear — fear that employees will make mistakes, or fear that it will take too long to explain the task. But failing to delegate traps supervisors in low-value work and prevents employees from growing.

Effective delegation requires:

- Matching the right task to the right employee.
- Clarifying the desired outcome, not micromanaging every step.
- Providing the necessary resources and authority.
- Following up with feedback and support.

Delegation multiplies productivity by creating shared ownership of results. It also ensures that knowledge is distributed rather than concentrated in the supervisor alone. A well-delegated team is more resilient, adaptable, and innovative.

Section 4 – Empowerment and Motivation

Productivity is not just about process — it is about people. Employees who feel empowered and motivated are far more productive than those who feel controlled or undervalued. Supervisors who foster ownership, recognize contributions, and involve employees in decision-making create an environment where people want to give their best.

Motivation is most effective when it connects daily tasks to larger meaning. Employees need to understand how their work contributes to organizational goals. Recognition plays a critical role. A simple acknowledgment of effort or progress can boost morale and inspire continued focus. Empowerment also requires trust. When supervisors trust employees to handle responsibilities, they free themselves to focus on leadership rather than micromanagement.

Section 5 – Enhancing Methodologies for Productivity

Supervisors have access to proven tools and methods to increase productivity:

- **Pareto Principle (80/20 Rule):** Focus on the 20% of tasks that generate 80% of results.

- **Lean Thinking:** Identify and eliminate waste in workflows.

- **Time Blocking:** Reserve uninterrupted blocks of time for priority tasks.

- **Kanban Boards and Dashboards:** Make progress visible and track accountability.

- **Checklists and Standard Operating Procedures: Ensure consistency** and reduce errors.

Supervisors should avoid overwhelming their teams with too many tools at once. Instead, please select one or two methods that align with the team's needs and apply them consistently. Even small changes can yield significant gains when applied with discipline.

Section 6 – The Role of Recognition in Productivity

Recognition is often overlooked as a driver of productivity. Employees who feel that their efforts are seen and appreciated are more likely to remain engaged and motivated. Recognition does not always require elaborate rewards. A timely thank-you, public acknowledgment, or personal note has the greatest impact.

Supervisors should also ask employees how they prefer to receive recognition. Some team members value public acknowledgment in front of peers, while others are more comfortable with private support and quiet affirmation. Respecting these preferences ensures recognition is meaningful rather than awkward.

Supervisors should make recognition part of their productivity strategy. For example, ending weekly meetings by highlighting specific contributions reinforces desired behaviors and builds morale. Recognition fosters a sense of progress and momentum, which directly fuels productivity.

Public Sector Case Snapshot

A supervisor at a state licensing office faced constant backlogs and rising frustration among staff. Employees were working hard but getting nowhere. The supervisor decided to address process and morale.

First, they introduced a standardized checklist to streamline case processing. Second, they delegated routine approvals to senior staff, freeing time for more complex work. Finally, they instituted a weekly recognition moment, where each employee's contributions were acknowledged.

The results were dramatic. Within four months, case completion rates increased by 30%, errors dropped sharply, and employee engagement scores rose. The combination of process improvement, delegation, and recognition turned a struggling team into a productive one.

Applied Tool – The Supervisor's Productivity Playbook

Use this two-part playbook to foster productivity on your team.

- Step 1: Diagnose Processes
    - Map workflows and identify bottlenecks.
    - Ask employees where they see wasted effort.
- Step 2: Delegate and Empower

- o   Assign tasks based on strengths.

- o   Provide authority along with responsibility.

- Step 3: Apply Productivity Tools

  - o   Select 1-2 methods (Pareto, Lean, Time Blocking).

  - o   Measure results after 30 days.

- Step 4: Recognize and Celebrate

  - o   Acknowledge progress publicly.

  - o   Highlight individual and team achievements.

- Step 5: Sustain and Refine

  - o   Build productivity reviews into regular meetings.

  - o   Adjust strategies as the team evolves.

Sample Team Productivity Scorecard

1. Key Outcomes Achieved (Yes/No).

2. Bottlenecks Addressed This Week.

3. Delegated Tasks Completed Without Escalation.

4. Employee Suggestions Implemented.

5. Recognition Moments Delivered.

This scorecard helps supervisors track not just activity but the drivers of true productivity.

Reflection Questions

1. Do I measure productivity by activity or by outcomes?

2. Where do I see the most wasted effort in our current processes?

3. What tasks should be delegated to increase team capacity?

4. How can I connect daily work to larger organizational goals?

5. Which productivity tool would most benefit my team right now?

6. Do I recognize employee contributions to productivity often?

7. Am I fostering ownership and accountability among employees?

8. What steps can I take to reduce bottlenecks in our workflows?

9. What would a well-orchestrated, highly productive team look like in my workplace?

Leadership-Centered Summary

Supervisors are not judged by how much they personally accomplish, but by the productivity of the teams they lead. Productivity requires orchestration — aligning people, processes, and priorities so that the whole is greater than the sum of its parts.

By redefining productivity as outcomes rather than activity, improving systems, delegating effectively, empowering employees, applying proven tools, and recognizing contributions, supervisors can unleash extraordinary results.

Think of yourself as a conductor. Your role is not to play every instrument but to bring harmony out of diversity. When you orchestrate well, the workplace shifts from noise to music — and productivity soars.

"Supervisors unleash productivity not by working harder themselves, but by orchestrating the efforts of many into a unified performance."

— Dr. Patrick C. Patrong

7 THE ARCHITECT OF TALENT

Crafting Excellence Through Onboarding

Introduction – First Impressions Last

Imagine starting a new job and being told, "Here's your desk. Good luck." That experience is more common than it should be, and it sets employees up for frustration and disengagement. Now picture a different scenario: on your first day, your supervisor greets you warmly, introduces you to your team, provides a roadmap of your first 90 days, and checks in regularly to support your success. Which environment is more likely to motivate, engage, and retain talent?

As a supervisor, you are the architect of onboarding. How you design the early experiences of new employees shapes their performance, loyalty, and perception of the organization. Research shows that employees who experience effective onboarding are 69% more likely to remain with an organization for at least three years. First impressions matter — and in supervision, they often last.

Section 1 – The Strategic Importance of Onboarding

Onboarding is more than orientation. Orientation may handle paperwork and policies, but onboarding is about integration. It ensures employees not only understand what they need to do but also how their role fits into the larger mission.

Effective onboarding leads to:

- Faster time to productivity.

- Greater employee engagement.

- Stronger alignment with organizational culture.

- Reduced turnover and recruitment costs.

Supervisors who neglect onboarding risk creating employees who feel disconnected, confused, or undervalued from the start. In contrast, supervisors who invest in onboarding build loyalty and set the foundation for excellence.

Section 2 – Designing an Effective Onboarding Experience

Supervisors must design onboarding with intentionality. A well-structured onboarding program includes three dimensions:

- **Administrative:** Completing essential paperwork, understanding policies, and receiving required training.

- **Operational:** Learning workflows, mastering tools, and shadowing experienced employees.

- **Cultural:** Building relationships, understanding team norms, and connecting to organizational values.

Onboarding should not be viewed as a one-day event but as a 90-day journey that gradually builds competence and confidence. New employees need structure and flexibility — clarity about expectations and opportunities to explore their role at their own pace.

Section 3 – The Role of Supervisors in Onboarding

Supervisors play a central role in onboarding because they translate organizational values into daily practice. HR can provide the paperwork, but supervisors provide the context.

Key responsibilities include:

- Welcoming the employee personally creates a sense of value

- Introducing the team and facilitating relationship-building.

- Setting clear goals for the first 30, 60, and 90 days.

- Checking in regularly to answer questions and provide feedback.

- Modeling the culture through daily interactions.

A supervisor's investment in these areas communicates one message loudly: you matter here. Employees who feel valued early are far more likely to stay and thrive.

Section 4 – Orienting Employees to Culture

Culture is often invisible but deeply influential. Supervisors are responsible for helping new employees understand not only policies and procedures but also the unwritten rules that guide how the team works.

This includes clarifying:

- **Communication styles** — how the team shares updates and information.

- **Decision-making norms** — who makes decisions and how input is valued.

- **Performance expectations** — what "good work" looks like.

- **Team rituals** — meetings, celebrations, or traditions that build cohesion.

Culture cannot be fully captured in a handbook. It must be experienced and explained. Supervisors who intentionally orient new employees to the culture accelerate integration and reduce confusion.

Section 5 – Training and Development in the Onboarding Process

Onboarding should include early development opportunities. Employees who feel they are learning and growing are more motivated to contribute.

Supervisors can:

- Provide structured training in essential skills.

- Pair new employees with mentors or "buddies."

- Encourage questions and create safe spaces for learning.

- Offer projects that allow new hires to show strengths.

Development is not only about technical training. It includes coaching in soft skills, guidance on navigating organizational politics, and encouragement to align personal goals with team objectives.

Section 6 – Continuous Improvement in Onboarding

The best onboarding processes evolve. Supervisors should seek feedback from recent hires about what worked, what was confusing, and what could be improved. By regularly refining onboarding, supervisors demonstrate adaptability and commitment to employee success.

Questions to ask new employees after their first 90 days:

- What was most helpful in your onboarding experience?

- Where did you feel unprepared?

- How can I better support future new hires?

Continuous improvement ensures that onboarding remains relevant, engaging, and effective.

Public Sector Case Snapshot

At a county human services agency, new employees were often overwhelmed by complex caseloads. Many resigned within the first year. Recognizing this pattern, the supervisor redesigned onboarding.

The new process included:

- A structured 90-day plan with clear milestones.

- Weekly check-ins to provide coaching and address concerns.

- A buddy system pairing new employees with experienced staff.

- Early exposure to the agency's mission with community visits.

The results were striking. Turnover decreased by 40% in the first year, employee confidence grew, and client satisfaction improved. The supervisor's investment in onboarding paid dividends not only for employees but also for the community they served.

Applied Tool – The 90-Day Onboarding Blueprint

Use this blueprint to design a structured onboarding journey:

- Days 1–30: Orientation and Connection

  o Complete administrative tasks.

  o Meet team members and establish relationships.

  o Clarify immediate responsibilities.

  o Shadow experienced employees.

- Days 31–60: Skill Building and Contribution

  o Receive training on systems and processes.

  o Begin independent projects with support.

  o Receive regular feedback.

  o Participate in team discussions and problem-solving.

- Days 61–90: Integration and Growth

  o Take ownership of core responsibilities.

  o Demonstrate contributions through completed projects.

  o Identify development goals for the next six months.

  o Provide feedback on the onboarding experience.

This blueprint ensures new employees feel supported, confident, and connected.

Reflection Questions

- How do I currently welcome new employees, and how might I improve the experience?

- Do I view onboarding as a one-day event or a 90-day journey?

- What cultural norms should I explain to new team members?

- How can I integrate training and development into onboarding?

- How do I personally play in making new employees feel valued?

- How can I use mentors or buddies to strengthen onboarding?

- What feedback have I gathered from past new hires, and how have I applied it?

- How does onboarding impact team morale and retention?

- If I were starting today, what would I want my supervisor to do differently?

Leadership-Centered Summary

Supervisors are not just managers of tasks — they are architects of talent. How you design and deliver onboarding sets the tone for an employee's entire journey. Effective onboarding is strategic, structured, and human-centered. It accelerates productivity, builds loyalty, and integrates employees into the culture.

Your influence as a supervisor begins the moment a new employee walks through the door. By investing in onboarding, you demonstrate care, vision, and leadership. First impressions matter — and as a supervisor, you have the power to make them count.

"Onboarding is not about filling a position; it is about building a foundation for excellence."

– Dr. Patrick C. Patrong

8 PERFORMANCE ALCHEMY
Turning Evaluation into Growth

Introduction – From Appraisal to Alchemy

Performance evaluations often arrive with a knot in the stomach. Employees brace for judgment; supervisors brace for difficult conversations. Too often, the process is treated as a once-a-year formality — a box to check rather than a lever for learning. But when handled well, evaluations become a catalyst for growth. They help people see their strengths clearly, confront gaps with courage, and map a path toward meaningful improvement.

A supervisor once told me, "I used to think evaluations were about ratings. Now I see they're about relationships." That shift — from grading to growing — is the essence of performance alchemy. In this chapter, you will learn how to turn assessment into development, feedback into momentum, and the evaluation meeting into the most constructive conversation of the year.

Section 1 – Rethinking the Purpose of Evaluation

Evaluation is not a verdict on the past; it is a springboard into the future. When employees view evaluation as punishment, they resist. When they experience it as partnership, they engage. Your task as a supervisor is to frame evaluation as a shared project: to recognize progress, clarify expectations, and co-create a plan for the next stage of growth.

At its best, evaluation serves four purposes:

- Provide clear, behavior-based feedback on results and impact.

- Recognize contributions and reinforce strengths with specifics.

- Identify skill or behavior gaps and the supports needed.

- Align individual goals with team objectives and organizational mission.

Keep the conversation developmental. Anchor observations in examples, not opinions. Link feedback to role expectations and outcomes. End every evaluation with forward motion — two or three clear goals, named resources, and dates for follow-up.

Section 2 – Preparing for the Evaluation Conversation

Great evaluations begin long before the meeting. Preparation communicates respect and builds credibility. It also reduces defensiveness because the conversation is grounded in facts, patterns, and shared expectations rather than surprise opinions.

Gather inputs from multiple angles:

- Performance data and work samples that show quality outcomes.

- Notes from one-on-ones, coaching moments, and prior check-ins throughout the year.

- Peer, client, or stakeholder feedback that illustrates collaboration and service.

- Self-assessment from the employee — ask them to identify wins, challenges, and goals.

Organize your evidence into themes: strengths that should be leveraged, gaps that must be addressed, and opportunities for stretch assignments. Prepare questions that invite reflection rather than trigger defensiveness. Plan the environment too — a private space, uninterrupted time, and a posture of partnership.

Section 3 – Conducting the Evaluation as a Dialogue

Evaluations work best as structured dialogues. Begin by setting a supportive tone: thank the employee for their work, outline the agenda, and reinforce the goal — to accelerate growth. Share observations succinctly, pausing to ask for the employee's perspective. The aim is not to 'deliver' a monologue but to build a shared, realistic picture of performance.

A dialogue-centered approach includes the following moves:

- Start with strengths first; name the behaviors and their impact on people, quality, and outcomes.

- Address growth areas with clarity and care — describe the behavior, the effect, and the expectation.

- Ask open questions: "What feels most challenging right now?" "Where do you want more support or stretch?"

- Co-create a small number of specific goals with timelines, measures, and supports.

Recognition belongs in the room too. Ask employees how they prefer to receive encouragement. Some thrive with public acknowledgment; others prefer private support. Tailoring recognition to preference increases its effectiveness and preserves trust.

Section 4 – Closing Gaps with Constructive Support

When a gap exists, employees need more than a warning — they need a map. The most effective supervisors pair accountability with support. Define the current state, describe the desired state, and specify the steps to get there. Agree on checkpoints, and follow through.

Use this simple pattern to structure improvement:

- Describe the gap with concrete examples and impact.

- Clarify the performance standard and its relation to the mission.

- Identify supports: training, shadowing, job aids, mentoring, or workload adjustments.

- Set timelines and interim milestones; schedule progress reviews in advance.

Document agreements in a concise development plan. Keep it visible. Reference it during one-on-ones so progress remains a shared project rather than a once-a-year surprise.

Section 5 – Sustaining Growth Beyond the Evaluation

The evaluation meeting is a milestone, not a finish line. Sustained growth depends on rhythm — recurring check-ins, regular recognition, and timely course corrections. Short, frequent conversations beat long, infrequent lectures. Your consistency builds safety; safety enables honest learning.

Sustain momentum with these practices:

- Hold quarterly development check-ins tied to goals set in the evaluation.

- Use one-on-ones to recognize progress, remove obstacles, and recalibrate priorities.

- Refresh goals as conditions change; growth plans should be living documents.

- Encourage self-tracking — ask employees to bring evidence of progress and questions for support.

Section 6 – The Supervisor as a Performance Coach

Think like a coach. Judges evaluate; coaches elevate. Coaching behaviors include asking powerful questions, noticing small wins, and aligning practice with purpose. When employees believe their supervisor is invested in their success, they take risks, seek feedback, and improve faster.

Practical coaching moves include:

- Use 'feedforward' — specific suggestions focused on the next attempt rather than the last mistake.

- Model the behavior you expect; let employees observe how you approach key tasks or conversations.

- Offer micro-learning: short demos, quick job aids, and five-minute practice moments embedded in the work.

- Celebrate progress publicly or privately based on preference, reinforcing effort and strategy as well as results.

Public Sector Case Snapshot

At a regional transportation division, annual evaluations had become a compliance ritual. Employees dreaded the season, and supervisors rushed through the forms. A newly appointed supervisor reframed the process. Two months before evaluation time, they began gathering multi-source feedback and scheduled pre-meetings to hear each employee's self-assessment. During the evaluation, they led with strengths, clarified two growth priorities, and co-authored development plans with resources and timelines.

The supervisor also normalized quarterly follow-ups and recognition moments tailored to preference — some team members appreciated a quick public shout-out in staff meetings, while others preferred a private note. Within a year, error rates dropped, project cycle times improved, and internal survey scores on 'my supervisor helps me grow' rose sharply. The culture shifted from appraisal anxiety to continuous improvement.

Applied Tool – The Performance Growth Framework

Use this four-step framework to turn evaluation into development:

Step 1: Prepare

o Gather performance evidence from multiple sources and time periods.

- o Summarize themes: strengths to leverage, gaps to close, opportunities to stretch.

- o Draft two or three coaching questions that invite reflection.

- Step 2: Dialogue

  - o Open with strengths and their impact; then address growth areas with candor and care.

  - o Ask about recognition preferences — public acknowledgment or private support — and tailor your approach.

  - o Co-create two or three SMART goals with clear metrics and dates.

- Step 3: Plan

  - o List specific supports: training modules, mentors, shadowing, tools, or workload shifts.

  - o Define checkpoints (30/60/90 days) and how progress will be evidenced.

  - o Capture agreements in a one-page plan accessible to both of you.

- Step 4: Follow-Up

  - o Hold quarterly growth check-ins; adjust goals as priorities evolve.

  - o Recognize progress frequently; remove barriers quickly.

  - o Renew the plan annually, carrying forward what works.

Reflection Questions

1. Do I frame evaluations as growth conversations or as compliance events?

2. How thoroughly do I prepare — what additional data or examples would strengthen my credibility?

3. Where might my feedback be too vague — how can I anchor it in observable behaviors and impact?

4. Which gaps require accountability and specific supports — what resources can I provide?

5. How will I sustain momentum after the meeting — what rhythm of check-ins will I commit to?

6. Have I asked each team member how they prefer recognition — public acknowledgment or private support?

7. What coaching behaviors will I practice to elevate performance?

8. How will I align individual goals with team outcomes so progress is visible and meaningful?

9. What one change could I make this evaluation season to increase trust and learning?

Leadership-Centered Summary

Performance alchemy is the supervisor's art of turning evaluation into growth. It rests on a partnership mindset, careful preparation, candid dialogue, and sustained follow-through. When employees trust that evaluations exist to help them excel, they lean into feedback and take ownership of improvement.

Lead as a coach who recognizes effort, clarifies standards, and equips people to meet them. When assessment fuels development, teams improve faster, morale rises, and results compound. That is the promise — and the practice — of performance alchemy.

"Performance alchemy is not about rating the past but about shaping the future."

Dr. Patrick C. Patrong

9 MASTERING THE ART OF CONNECTION
Communicating for Success

Introduction – Communication as the Cornerstone of Leadership

Communication is the supervisor's most important tool. Without it, expectations remain unclear, conflicts go unresolved, and trust erodes. With it, teams thrive, relationships strengthen, and productivity accelerates. Supervisors who master communication create a culture where people know what to do, why it matters, and how they are valued.

I recall a supervisor who struggled because employees never seemed aligned. Instructions were vague, updates inconsistent, and feedback rare. Frustration mounted until they learned to prioritize clear, consistent, and empathetic communication. The transformation was dramatic: morale improved, output stabilized, and the team began to trust their leader. This chapter explores how supervisors can communicate to connect, resolve, and inspire.

Section 1 – Building Trust Through Active Listening

Listening is more than waiting for your turn to talk. Active listening builds trust because it makes people feel heard and respected. When supervisors listen carefully, employees open up, share concerns earlier, and engage more fully in solutions.

Practical listening strategies include:

- Maintain eye contact and minimize distractions during conversations.

- Reflect back what you hear to confirm understanding: "So what you're saying is…"

- Validate feelings even when you cannot agree with every point: "I can see this is frustrating for you."

- Ask clarifying questions rather than making assumptions.

Trust is the currency of supervision, and listening is the transaction that builds it. When employees know their voices matter, they extend trust in return.

Section 2 – Clarity and Consistency in Everyday Communication

Employees need clarity. Ambiguity leads to confusion, wasted effort, and frustration. Supervisors must ensure their words are simple, direct, and consistent across settings.

Tips for ensuring clarity and consistency:

- State expectations plainly — avoid jargon or assumptions that employees 'just know.'

- Repeat key messages through multiple channels (meetings, emails, one-on-ones).

- Align words with actions — consistency between what you say and what you do reinforces credibility.

- Check for understanding: ask employees to restate key points to confirm clarity.

Consistency is leadership's credibility test. If your communication shifts unpredictably, employees lose trust. Clear, steady communication anchors the team.

Section 3 – Handling Difficult Conversations

Every supervisor must have difficult conversations — about performance, behavior, or conflict. Avoiding them only makes problems grow. The key is preparation, tone, and a focus on solutions rather than blame.

Steps for handling difficult conversations:

- Prepare: Gather facts, examples, and desired outcomes before the meeting.

- Set the environment: Choose a private, respectful space free from interruptions.

- Open with purpose: State clearly why the conversation is happening and what you hope to achieve.

- Explore together: Ask the employee's perspective and listen actively.

- Agree on actions: Define specific next steps and supports.

- Follow up: Schedule a check-in to review progress and reinforce accountability.

Handled well, difficult conversations can strengthen relationships rather than damage them. They show employees you care enough to address issues honestly.

Section 4 – Communication that Motivates and Inspires

Supervisors must also use communication to energize. Recognition, storytelling, and connecting daily work to larger purpose inspire people to give their best. Motivational communication is less about speeches and more about genuine moments that connect effort to meaning.

Ways supervisors can inspire through communication:

- Recognize contributions in real time — thank employees specifically for what they did and its impact.

- Tell stories that illustrate values and vision, making abstract goals tangible.

- Share the 'why' behind tasks, not just the 'what' and 'how.'

- Use positive language that highlights possibility rather than limitation.

When communication carries inspiration, employees feel not only directed but valued. This sense of meaning drives engagement and performance.

Section 5 – Adapting to Different Styles

Not every employee receives communication the same way. Some prefer detailed instructions; others want freedom to explore. Some value frequent feedback; others find it overwhelming. Effective supervisors adapt their communication style to meet diverse needs.

Consider these adaptations:

- Use personality assessments or informal observations to learn preferences.

- Adjust detail level: provide step-by-step guidance for some, broad goals for others.

- Flex between written and verbal communication depending on the employee's strengths.

- Balance frequency — some employees thrive on frequent check-ins; others value autonomy.

Adaptability shows respect. It communicates that you value employees as individuals and are willing to meet them where they are.

Public Sector Case Snapshot

At a municipal housing department, communication breakdowns plagued a team. Instructions were unclear, feedback was inconsistent, and employees often felt blindsided by criticism. One supervisor decided to focus on mastering communication. They began each week with a short team huddle to clarify priorities, practiced active listening in one-on-ones, and adopted a framework for handling difficult conversations.

The impact was immediate. Employees reported greater trust, fewer misunderstandings, and a stronger sense of teamwork. Productivity rose because people knew what was expected, and conflicts were addressed quickly rather than festering. The supervisor's deliberate investment in communication transformed relationships and results.

Applied Tool – Difficult Conversation Framework

Use this framework to guide high-stakes conversations:

Step 1: Prepare

- Clarify the purpose and desired outcome.
- Gather facts, examples, and evidence.
- Plan your opening statement and questions.

Step 2: Open

- State the issue clearly and respectfully.
- Explain why the conversation is necessary.
- Set a collaborative tone from the start.

Step 3: Explore

- Invite the employee's perspective; listen without interruption.
- Acknowledge feelings and clarify misunderstandings.
- Look for common ground and shared goals.

Step 4: Agree

- Identify specific actions, supports, and timelines.
- Ensure supervisor and employee agree on the plan.
- Document commitments to reinforce accountability.

Step 5: Follow-Up

- Schedule a progress review to check results.

- Recognize improvements and adjust support as needed.

- Keep the door open for continued dialogue.

Reflection Questions

1. How well do I practice active listening with my employees?

2. Are my expectations clear and easy to understand?

3. How do I handle difficult conversations?

4. Do I use recognition and storytelling to inspire my team?

5. Can I adapt my communication style for different employees?

6. Do I check for understanding rather than assume clarity?

7. Do my words and actions consistently match?

8. How do I prepare for high-stakes conversations in advance?

9. How will I strengthen my supervisory communication?

Leadership-Centered Summary

Communication is the supervisor's art of connection. It builds trust, ensures clarity, resolves conflict, and inspires performance. When supervisors master communication, they multiply their influence because employees not only hear the words but feel the intent behind them.

By listening actively, speaking clearly, addressing challenges directly, inspiring through recognition and meaning, and adapting to diverse styles, supervisors turn communication into a cornerstone of leadership success. Connection is not optional; it is the channel through which all supervision flows.

"Supervisors lead best when they master the art of connection — communicating not just to be heard, but to be understood." — Dr. Patrick C. Patrong

10 COACHING, COUNSELING, AND MENTORING
The Supervisor's Compass

Introduction – The Compass of Guidance

Supervision is more than assigning tasks and tracking results. It is guiding people — through uncertainty, through challenge, and toward potential. Three approaches form the supervisor's compass: coaching, counseling, and mentoring. Each point in a different direction, and the wisdom of leadership is knowing which direction to choose, when to switch, and how to integrate them so that employees feel supported, accountable, and inspired.

Consider the story of Lena, a new supervisor inheriting a high-stakes project team. One analyst, brilliant but blunt, delivered strong work yet left colleagues wary. Another employee missed deadlines after a family crisis. A third was eager, capable, and hungry for growth. Lena learned quickly that a single approach would not suffice. She coached the analyst on influence and stakeholder management; she counseled the employee in crisis with empathy, resources, and structure; and she mentored the eager staffer, opening doors to cross-functional opportunities. Within months, the team stabilized, the project met milestones, and engagement improved because Lena led with a compass — not a one-size-fits-all tool.

This chapter gives you that compass. You will clarify the distinctions among coaching, counseling, and mentoring; practice when and how to apply them; and leave with a practical framework, scripts, and measures you can use immediately.

Section 1 – Distinguishing Coaching, Counseling, and Mentoring

Precision matters. When we blur these approaches, we confuse expectations and dilute impact. Use the following distinctions to select the right path.

- **Coaching:** Short-to-mid term, performance-focused conversations that unlock capability through questions, practice, and feedback.

- **Counseling:** Supportive, boundary-aware problem-solving when personal stressors or conflicts impede work performance or behavior.

- **Mentoring:** Long-term, relationship-based guidance on career direction, identity as a professional, networks, and strategic growth.

Think of the three as lenses. Coaching zooms in on a specific skill or goal. Counseling clears the fog when life events cloud performance. Mentoring zooms out to the broader arc of a career. Skilled supervisors move among these lenses intentionally rather than accidentally.

Section 2 – Coaching for Performance

Coaching improves a defined performance outcome. The supervisor's stance is curious, candid, and catalytic — asking questions that spark insight, offering targeted feedback, and creating a low-risk practice environment.

A simple rhythm you can use is the GROW model:

- **Goal** – Clarify the specific result to achieve and why it matters now.

- **Reality** – Explore current behaviors, evidence, constraints, and strengths.

- **Options** – Generate multiple approaches; compare tradeoffs; select a path.

- **Will** – Define concrete next steps, timing, and support; confirm commitment.

Effective coaching conversations are short, frequent, and specific. Replace vague advice ("be more proactive") with observable behaviors ("bring two solution options with each issue by Wednesday"). Close by agreeing how progress will be measured and when you will review it.

Coaching micro-skills to practice:

- Ask one more question before you offer advice — it surfaces assumptions and builds ownership.

- Use feedforward: offer suggestions for the next attempt rather than replaying the last mistake.

- Normalize iteration: frame skill-building as drafts and reps, not as pass/fail judgments.

Section 3 – Counseling for Challenges

Counseling is appropriate when non-technical barriers are undermining work — stress, conflict, health, grief, or ethical concerns. Supervisors are not clinicians, but they are first-line supporters. The aim is to acknowledge the reality, connect the employee to resources, and re-establish a workable plan with clear expectations.

Practical counseling steps:

- Create privacy and psychological safety; signal care and neutrality.

- Name observed impacts factually ("I've noticed three late reports this month").

- Invite the employee's perspective; listen for root causes without prying.

- Offer resources (e.g., EAP, schedule flexibility, workload adjustments) and clarify boundaries and confidentiality.

- Co-create a near-term plan that balances compassion with accountability, with dates to review.

    Boundary language you can use:

- "I'm here to support your success at work. I'm not a counselor, and I want to connect you to resources that can help."

- "Let's define what success looks like over the next two weeks and what support would make that possible."

Document agreements succinctly. Follow up promptly. If conduct or performance doesn't improve, escalate through your formal process — support and accountability go together.

Section 4 – Mentoring for Growth

Mentoring is an investment in the future. It sends a powerful message: "You belong here, and we see your potential." Supervisors can mentor directly or broker mentors elsewhere in the organization.

High-impact mentoring practices:

- Share decision-making logic, not just decisions, to develop judgment.

- Provide calibrated stretch assignments with safety nets and debriefs.

- Open networks: make warm introductions and advocate (sponsorship) when appropriate.

- Practice reverse mentoring: invite junior staff to teach you emerging tools and perspectives — it dignifies their expertise and accelerates your learning.

Mentoring conversations are future-facing: values, aspirations, identity, and pathways. They help employees connect daily work to a larger narrative of growth.

Section 5 – Integrating the Three Approaches

Supervisory excellence is diagnostic. Ask yourself: What is the primary need right now — performance skill, personal stability, or long-term development? Choose accordingly, then blend as conditions change.

A simple decision guide:

- Is the gap a skill or execution issue? → Start with Coaching.

- Is the gap driven by personal stress or conflict? → Start with Counseling.

- Is the conversation about aspirations and future paths? → Start with Mentoring.

Illustrative scenarios:

- Analyst misses stakeholder deadlines due to weak planning → Coach using GROW; later Mentor on managing cross-functional relationships.

- Strong performer's tone shuts others down → Coach on feedback delivery; Mentor on influence; Counsel if conflict escalates.

- New hire eager to advance → Mentor on pathways; Coach on present-role mastery; Counsel only if personal barriers arise.

Section 6 – Measuring Impact of Your Compass

What gets measured improves. Track leading and lagging indicators to see whether your use of coaching, counseling, and mentoring is working.

Leading indicators (early signals):

- Frequency of one-on-ones and coaching touchpoints.

- Completion of development actions (courses, shadowing, job aids created).

- Psychological safety signals (idea sharing, questions asked).

  Lagging indicators (results over time):

- Quality, timeliness, and error rates on key deliverables.

- Retention and internal movement (promotions, lateral growth).

- Engagement pulse items (e.g., "My supervisor helps me grow").

Public Sector Case Snapshot

In a county public health lab, turnaround times were slipping and tensions ran high. The supervisor mapped issues to the compass: two technicians needed skill coaching on a new instrument; one senior analyst faced caregiving stress; and a promising coordinator sought a development path.

The supervisor implemented weekly 20-minute coaching sprints using GROW for the technicians, scheduled a counseling conversation with the analyst that connected them to schedule flexibility and EAP, and launched a mentoring plan with stretch assignments for the coordinator alongside visibility with cross-agency partners.

Ninety days later, rework dropped by 35%, turnaround times met targets three weeks in a row, the analyst stabilized attendance, and the coordinator co-led a process improvement that saved dozens of staff hours monthly. The magic was not a single program; it was the supervisor's compass, applied with consistency.

Applied Tool – The Supervisor's Compass Framework (Expanded)

Use this six-step framework with scripts you can adapt:

Step 1: Diagnose

- Define the presenting issue in observable terms (behavior, impact, examples, dates).

- Ask: Is this primarily a skill gap, a personal barrier, or a growth question?

Step 2: Choose

- Select Coaching, Counseling, or Mentoring as the primary mode for this conversation.

- Decide what secondary mode may follow (e.g., Coach now, Mentor next month).

Step 3: Contract

- Set the purpose, roles, and timebox: "Let's spend 20 minutes to clarify the skill and practice two approaches."

- Confirm confidentiality limits when counseling; set expectations for documentation when coaching performance.

Step 4: Act (by Mode)

- Coaching — Use GROW; agree on two behaviors to try before next check-in; provide a job aid or model a rep.

- Counseling — Share observations and impact; offer resources; co-create a short, realistic plan; set a review date.

- Mentoring — Explore aspirations; map pathways; broker a connection; assign a stretch task with a debrief.

Step 5: Document

- Capture agreements on one page: goals, actions, support, dates, and success evidence. Share a copy.

Step 6: Review

- Hold a brief follow-up; recognize progress; adjust or escalate if commitments are not met.

Do / Don't Essentials

- Do tailor your stance; Don't use the same tool for every problem.

- Do ask recognition preferences (public or private); Don't assume everyone wants the same support.

- Do pair accountability with aid; Don't let empathy erase expectations.

- Do model learning; Don't present perfection — show your own growth mindset.

Reflection Questions

1. When I face a people challenge, do I pause to diagnose before I act?

2. Which mode (coaching, counseling, mentoring) do I overuse — and which do I underuse? Why?

3. What coaching questions reliably unlock insight for my team?

4. How can I make counseling conversations compassionate while keeping expectations clear?

5. Whom am I mentoring right now — and who needs a mentor I could broker?

6. How will I measure the impact of my compass over the next quarter?

7. Where can I add short, frequent coaching touchpoints instead of long, infrequent meetings?

8. What boundaries and resources should I prepare in advance for counseling?

9. Which stretch assignments could accelerate growth for ready employees?

10. How will I tailor recognition (public or private) to each person's preference?

11. What's one script from this chapter I will try this week?

12. If my team adopted the compass mindset, what would be different three months from now?

Leadership-Centered Summary

Great supervisors do not rely on a single tool. They navigate. By diagnosing needs and choosing among coaching, counseling, and mentoring, you create a humane, high-performance environment where people feel seen, supported, and stretched. The compass keeps you from overcorrecting — too soft or too hard — and guides you to the next right conversation.

Adopt the rhythm: diagnose, choose, contract, act, document, review. Celebrate progress in the open or in private, as each employee prefers. As you practice, your team will feel the shift: fewer surprises, more clarity, faster growth, and stronger results. That is the promise of a supervisor who leads with a compass — not a hammer.

"The supervisor's compass is not found in a single tool but in the wisdom to know when to coach, when to counsel, and when to mentor."

— Dr. Patrick C. Patrong.

11 LEADING CHANGE IN A SHIFTING WORLD
:
Introduction – The Challenge of Change

Change is inevitable in every organization. New policies, technologies, and priorities constantly reshape the workplace. For supervisors, leading change is an opportunity and a test of leadership. How you guide employees through uncertainty determines whether change sparks growth or resistance.

Consider a supervisor in a government agency tasked with implementing a new digital system. Employees feared job loss, complained about complexity, and questioned the need for change. Instead of imposing directives, the supervisor communicated openly, involved employees in training, and celebrated small milestones. Within six months, adoption exceeded expectations and morale improved. This story illustrates the power of leading change with clarity, empathy, and persistence.

Section 1 – Understanding the Nature of Change

Change is not just external; it is emotional. Employees often experience denial, fear, or frustration before acceptance. Supervisors must anticipate these reactions and normalize them as part of the process.

Key insights:

- Change disrupts routines and comfort zones, triggering resistance.

- Employees progress through stages: awareness, resistance, exploration, and commitment.

- Supervisors accelerate adaptation by providing information, support, and involvement.

Recognizing change as a human journey equips supervisors to respond with patience and intentionality rather than frustration.

Section 2 – Preparing for Change

Preparation is critical. Change efforts fail when supervisors underestimate planning. Employees need a roadmap that explains the what, why, and how.

Preparation steps:

- Clarify the purpose: Why is the change happening and what problem does it solve?

- Identify stakeholders: Who is most affected and how will they be engaged?

- Develop a communication plan: What will be shared, when, and through what channels?

- Anticipate obstacles: Where is resistance likely and how will you address it?

Preparation builds credibility. When supervisors present a thoughtful plan, employees trust the process more and resist less.

Section 3 – Communicating Through Change

Communication is the lifeline of change. Silence breeds rumors, while transparency fosters trust. Supervisors should over-communicate during transitions, using multiple channels and reinforcing messages consistently.

Effective communication practices include:

- Explain the rationale behind the change clearly and frequently.

- Acknowledge concerns honestly without minimizing them.

- Share progress updates and celebrate small wins.

- Invite feedback and respond visibly to employee input.

When communication is clear, employees feel respected and are more likely to commit to the new direction.

Section 4 – Involving Employees in the Process

Employees support what they help create. Involvement transforms resistance into ownership. Supervisors should seek input on implementation and empower employees to shape solutions.

Practical strategies:

- Form task forces or pilot groups to test new processes.

- Invite employees to suggest adaptations that fit their workflows.

- Use workshops or forums to gather insights and answer questions.

- Recognize contributions publicly to reinforce ownership.

When employees see their fingerprints on the change, they become champions rather than critics.

Section 5 – Supporting Employees Through Transition

Change creates stress. Supervisors must provide emotional and practical support. Offering resources demonstrates care and helps employees adapt faster.

Support strategies:

- Provide training tailored to employee needs and skill levels.

- Offer coaching and one-on-one check-ins to address concerns.

- Encourage peer support through mentoring or buddy systems.

- Promote resilience by acknowledging progress and encouraging balance.

Support signals to employees that they are not alone in the transition, strengthening trust and commitment.

Section 6 – Sustaining Change Over Time

The real test of change leadership is sustainability. Without reinforcement, employees drift back to old habits. Supervisors must institutionalize new practices and maintain momentum.

Sustainability practices:

- Monitor progress with clear metrics and adjust as needed.

- Integrate new practices into performance goals and evaluations.

- Celebrate milestones and acknowledge persistence.

- Continue to solicit feedback and refine processes.

Sustained change requires vigilance. Supervisors who reinforce new behaviors ensure that improvements endure.

Public Sector Case Snapshot

At a state transportation department, a supervisor was tasked with implementing new safety protocols. Employees initially resisted, citing extra workload. The supervisor communicated the reasons, formed a task force to pilot changes, and recognized early adopters. Over time, employees embraced the protocols, accidents declined, and safety culture strengthened. The supervisor's leadership turned resistance into success.

Applied Tool – The Change Leadership Framework

Use this six-step framework to guide change:

Step 1: Prepare

- Clarify purpose, stakeholders, and potential obstacles.

Step 2: Communicate

- Over-communicate with transparency and consistency.

Step 3: Involve

- Engage employees in planning and implementation.

Step 4: Support

- Provide training, coaching, and resources.

Step 5: Monitor

- Track progress with clear metrics and feedback loops.

Step 6: Celebrate

- Recognize milestones and sustain momentum.

Reflection Questions

1. How do I typically respond to change — with openness or resistance?

2. What communication strategies can I use to reduce fear during transitions?

3. How can I involve employees more effectively in shaping change?

4. What support systems do I have to help employees adapt?

5. How do I monitor and reinforce change after implementation?

6. What small wins can I celebrate to maintain momentum?

7. How do I respond to resistance constructively rather than defensively?

8. What lessons from past changes can I apply to future efforts?

9. How can I model adaptability as a supervisor?

10. What would it look like for my team to view change as an opportunity rather than a threat?

Leadership-Centered Summary

Change will always challenge organizations, but supervisors who lead with clarity, involvement, and empathy turn disruption into growth. By preparing thoughtfully, communicating consistently, supporting employees, and sustaining momentum, supervisors build resilient teams capable of thriving in shifting landscapes.

"Supervisors who lead change with clarity and care transform uncertainty into opportunity."

— Dr. Patrick C. Patrong

12 DISCIPLINE FOR SUCCESS
A Blueprint for Supervisorship

Introduction – Discipline as Leadership, Not Punishment

Discipline has a branding problem. Too many supervisors equate it with punishment and confrontation, while too many employees experience it as arbitrary or unfair. In reality, discipline is simply the practice of aligning behavior with standards so that people can work well together. It is clarity over confusion, consistency over favoritism, and growth over grudges. When supervisors embrace discipline as leadership, teams experience order, safety, and respect — the conditions where excellence can flourish.

Consider a real scenario from a public agency benefits office. A high-volume clerk, Jamal, began arriving late three to four times each week. His supervisor, already stretched thin, let it slide for weeks to avoid a difficult conversation. Morale slipped. Peers started to ask why standards didn't apply equally. When the supervisor finally acted, he framed discipline as support: he clarified expectations, documented incidents, explored root causes (childcare transportation), and agreed to a temporary schedule adjustment with clear checkpoints. Within a month, attendance stabilized, backlogs declined, and the team's trust in leadership improved.

This chapter provides a practical blueprint to apply discipline with fairness, empathy, and precision. You will learn how to set expectations that stick, use progressive discipline step-by-step, document decisively, and prevent many issues through proactive leadership. Scripts, checklists, and a model corrective action plan are included so you can apply the ideas immediately.

Section 1 – Redefining Discipline

Reframing discipline begins with language. Replace punitive framing ("I'm writing you up") with developmental framing ("I'm responsible for helping you meet the standard"). Accountability is not the opposite of compassion; it is how compassion protects the whole team. Discipline fails when it is delayed, uneven, or undocumented. It succeeds when it is timely, consistent, and clear.

What disciplined leadership is — and is not:

- It is clarity about the standard, the behavior observed, and the impact on people, safety, quality, or service.

- It is a fair chance to improve with support and timelines.

- It is documentation that preserves facts and reduces bias.

- It is not venting, shaming, or surprising employees with new expectations.

- It is not one-size-fits-all; the response matches severity, frequency, and risk.

The purpose of discipline is to restore performance and trust. Even when separation becomes necessary, a dignified process reduces harm to people and culture.

Section 2 – Establishing Clear Expectations

Many discipline issues are really expectation issues. Employees cannot hit a target they cannot see. Make the standard visible, specific, and tied to mission and values.

Build an expectation statement with four elements:

- **Standard** – the specific requirement ("Reports are due by 3:00 p.m. each Friday").

- **Rationale** – why it matters ("Finance closes on Fridays; late reports delay client payments").

- **Evidence** – how it's measured ("Timestamp in the reporting portal").

- **Support** – resources or job aids available ("Template, checklist, and office hours on Thursdays").

Sample script for setting expectations in a team meeting:

"Starting this month, weekly case updates are due by 3:00 p.m. on Fridays because Finance runs payroll at 4:00. You'll use the updated template in the portal — it time-stamps submissions. If you hit a roadblock, bring it to Thursday's office hours so we can solve it before the deadline."

Reinforce expectations in writing (email, SOPs, shared drive) and in rhythm (onboarding, 1:1s, huddles). Consistency beats intensity — small, frequent reminders prevent big, painful corrections.

Section 3 – The Progressive Discipline Pathway

Progressive discipline escalates only as needed, giving employees a fair chance to improve while protecting standards. The steps below include scripts to help you speak with clarity and respect.

Step 1: Clarify (Informal Conversation)

- Goal: Restate the standard; surface obstacles; agree on immediate next steps.

- Script: "I've noticed X on [dates]. The standard is Y because Z. What's getting in the way? Let's agree on the next two steps to get you back on track by [date]."

Step 2: Coach (Documented Coaching/Verbal Warning)

- Goal: Provide feedback, practice new behaviors, and set a short review window.

- Script: "To meet the standard, here are two specific behaviors I need to see. Let's practice them now. We'll check progress in one week on [date]. I'll document what we agreed."

Step 3: Document (Written Warning)

- Goal: Record facts, expectations, resources, and consequences for non-improvement.

- Script: "This letter summarizes the pattern observed, the standard, the supports provided, and the improvement required by [date]. Future incidents may lead to additional action."

Step 4: Correct (Final Warning or Suspension, per policy)

- Goal: Communicate seriousness; provide one last, specific chance to meet standards.

- Script: "Given the continued issues, this is a final warning. To continue in this role, you must achieve X by [date]. Here are the supports available. We will review on [date]."

Step 5: Decide (Separation or Reassignment)

- Goal: Apply policy fairly when standards are not met despite support.

- Script: "We have not seen the required improvement. In accordance with policy section __, we are moving to [action]. HR will provide the next steps."

Always follow your jurisdiction's policy and consult HR/Legal on language and steps. Progressive discipline is a fairness practice and a due-process safeguard.

Section 4 – Balancing Accountability and Empathy

Accountability without empathy feels punitive; empathy without accountability feels unfair. The balance builds trust. Use tone, body language, and words that convey firmness and care.

Practical techniques:

- Name the value and the standard: "I care about your success and our clients' safety. That's why this standard matters."

- Acknowledge emotion: "I can hear your frustration. Let's focus on the steps we can take this week."

- Offer choices: "Would job aids or shadowing help more for the next two reports?"

- Set a near-term checkpoint: "Let's talk next Tuesday to review two examples."

Remember to ask for preference for recognition and support: some employees appreciate public acknowledgment of improvement; others prefer private conversations.

Section 5 – Documentation and Due Process

If it isn't written, it didn't happen. Documentation protects employees and supervisors by preserving facts, timelines, and support offered. Keep records objective, specific, and secure.

Checklist for a solid written record:

- Dates, times, and descriptions of observed behaviors (objective facts).

- The standard or policy with citations (what good looks like).

- Employee's explanation or context (what you heard).

- Supports offered (training, schedule adjustment, tools).

- Expectations for improvement (specific behaviors, by when, how measured).

Due process means the employee understands the concern, has a chance to respond, and receives a fair opportunity to improve. Apply the same process equitably across cases to avoid bias.

Section 6 – Preventing Discipline Through Proactive Leadership

The easiest discipline conversation is the one you never need. Prevention comes from culture: clear expectations, steady feedback, peer support, and timely recognition.

Prevention moves to put on repeat:

- Weekly 1:1s for priorities, roadblocks, and recognition.

- Two-way SOP reviews so employees help refine standards they must meet.

- Peer mentoring for early skill gaps and new processes.

- Recognition cadence (public or private per preference) to reinforce desired behaviors.

- Early alerts: address slippage within 48 hours to avoid patterns.

Supervisors who invest in prevention spend less time in formal discipline and more time developing people.

Section 7 – Special Situations Requiring Extra Care

Some issues require heightened coordination with HR and adherence to policies. Use caution and consult early in the following scenarios.

- **Attendance and leave**: Align with policy and applicable laws; document patterns and conversations precisely.

- **Safety or harassment**: Prioritize immediate safety; involve HR/Legal; follow investigative protocols.

- **Falsification or misconduct**: Preserve evidence and confidentiality; escalate promptly per policy.

- **Union environments**: Respect contract provisions (representation rights, timelines, notice).

- **Remote/hybrid employees**: Define availability, response times, and documentation expectations explicitly.

In sensitive cases, your tone still matters: dignity and neutrality reduce defensiveness and risk while reinforcing fairness.

Public Sector Case Snapshot

In a county facilities division, equipment checkouts were frequently late or missing, delaying field crews. The supervisor analyzed the logs, identified two recurring patterns, and launched a targeted response. First, she reset expectations at a team huddle and followed up with a written SOP and a laminated checklist at the cage. She then met individually with two employees: one needed coaching on planning and reminders; the other admitted to skipping steps to "save time." After a documented coaching period with weekly check-ins, one employee improved. The other continued to miss scans despite support, prompting a written warning and, later, a final warning.

Within 60 days, late returns dropped 70%, and the on-time departure of field crews increased. The team reported higher fairness in the annual survey, citing consistent standards and clear communication. Discipline, done well, improves performance and morale.

Applied Tool – The Progressive Discipline Blueprint

This tool, with scripts and evidence prompts, can guide your actions.

1. Clarify

- State the data: "On 9/2, 9/7, and 9/12, reports were submitted after the 3:00 p.m. deadline."

- Restate the standard and rationale. Ask, "What's getting in the way?" Capture obstacles without judgment.

2. Coach

- Define two behaviors to practice before the next check-in; provide a job aid or model an example.

- Script: "Let's try blocking 30 minutes on Fridays and using the checklist. I'll check back next Tuesday."

3. Document

- Summarize the pattern, standard, supports, and the improvement required (who/what/when/how measured).

- Store a dated copy; share per policy; invite the employee's written response if desired.

4. Correct

- Escalate per policy; be specific about the final chance and the timeline.

- Ensure the employee understands potential consequences and available supports.

5. Decide

- If improvement is not achieved, apply the next policy step with HR guidance; maintain dignity in delivery.

6. Follow Up & Reinforce

- Recognize sustained improvement (publicly or privately per preference). Remove unnecessary monitoring once stability returns.

Model Corrective Action Plan (one page)

- Concern/Standard: _____

- Evidence/Dates: _____

- Employee Context: _____
- Supports Provided: _____
- Required Behaviors: _____
- Measurement & Timeline: _____
- Consequences if Not Met: _____
- Check-in Dates/Outcomes: _____

Reflection Questions

1. Where have I delayed discipline, and what did it cost the team?

2. Which expectations in my area need to be rewritten for clarity and measurability?

3. What phrase will I use to frame discipline as support rather than punishment?

4. Which step of progressive discipline do I often skip— and why?

5. How will I document more objectively (dates, behaviors, impact) starting this week?

6. What supports can I standardize (job aids, templates, office hours) to make improvement easier?

7. How will I calibrate my tone to convey empathy and accountability?

8. What recognition cadence will I use to reinforce improved behavior (public or private)?

9. Which special situations require pre-coordination with HR?

10. What early-warning signals (metrics or behaviors) will I watch to intervene sooner?

11. Where might bias creep into my discipline decisions, and how will I counter it?

12. What will my one-page corrective action plan template include?

13. How will I close the loop with the team to reinforce fairness without breaching confidentiality?

14. In what ways will I model disciplined leadership for other supervi**sors?**

Leadership-Centered Summary

Discipline, practiced as leadership, stabilizes culture and performance. Your fairness signals safety; your consistency earns credibility; your documentation protects everyone. Most importantly, your combination of empathy and accountability helps people improve — which is the purpose of discipline in a mission-driven organization.

Lead with clarity, act with timeliness, and follow through with integrity. Recognize progress in a way each employee prefers. When standards are visible and lived, teams thrive — and discipline becomes a quiet, steady force for good.

"Discipline is not the absence of compassion but the presence of accountability."
— *Dr. Patrick C. Patrong.*

13 RESOLVING CHALLENGES WITH GRACE
Navigating Employee Concerns

Introduction – Grace Under Pressure

Every supervisor will face employee concerns — ranging from interpersonal conflicts to workload stress, from misunderstandings to performance disputes. How a supervisor responds in these moments defines their credibility and shapes team culture. Some leaders react defensively or harshly, escalating issues further. Others avoid problems altogether, allowing resentment to fester. The most effective supervisors, however, resolve challenges with grace. They listen with patience, respond with fairness, and create pathways to solutions that strengthen trust rather than weaken it.

Consider the example of a supervisor in a large city agency who faced an employee grievance about workload distribution. Rather than dismissing the concern or reacting with frustration, the supervisor invited the employee to share details, reviewed workload data, and convened a discussion with the team. The process revealed miscommunication rather than malice. By handling the issue transparently and respectfully, the supervisor not only resolved the concern but also built stronger team cohesion.

This chapter provides practical strategies for supervisors to address employee concerns without losing authority or damaging relationships. You will learn how to listen with empathy, apply fairness consistently, manage emotions during tense conversations, and build collaborative solutions. A framework, case snapshot, and reflection tools are included to help you respond with clarity and compassion.

Section 1 – Understanding the Nature of Employee Concerns

Employee concerns rarely emerge in isolation. They often signal deeper issues in communication, fairness, or culture. A supervisor's job is to interpret not just the words spoken, but the underlying needs being expressed. Concerns may be rational, emotional, or both. Treating them only as complaints to dismiss wastes valuable insight.

Common categories of concerns include:

- Workload distribution and fairness of assignments.

- Interpersonal conflicts between colleagues or between employee and supervisor.

- Perceptions of favoritism, inequity, in decision-making.

- Unclear expectations, shifting goals, or inconsistent communication.

- Personal challenges of employees and supervisors that spill into workplace performance.

- Lack of recognition or feedback that leaves employees feeling undervalued or disconnected.

When supervisors identify patterns, they can address systemic issues that prevent concerns from recurring. Each concern is a challenge and an opportunity to improve the workplace.

Section 2 – Listening as the First Step to Resolution

Listening is not passive — it is an active demonstration of respect.

Employees who feel heard are more willing to accept outcomes, even unfavorable ones. Listening communicates that the employee's perspective has value.

Practical listening skills include:

- Allowing the employee to speak without interruption, even if you disagree.

- Paraphrasing key points to confirm shared understanding.

- Asking clarifying questions to uncover underlying issues.

- Acknowledging emotions as legitimate, even if facts differ.

- Taking notes to demonstrate seriousness and capture commitments.

Supervisors who discipline themselves to listen before speaking reduce defensiveness, uncover important context, and model professionalism for the team.

Section 3 – Responding with Fairness and Consistency

Fairness is the cornerstone of trust. Employees evaluate every response not only for themselves but as a signal of how others will be treated. Inconsistent responses create perceptions of favoritism and erode credibility.

Guidelines for fair responses:

- Investigate facts carefully before making decisions.

- Apply policies consistently across individuals and situations.

- Document actions and outcomes for transparency and accountability.

- Explain decisions and the reasoning behind them clearly to all parties.

Fairness does not always mean identical outcomes, but it does mean transparent standards and equal treatment under those standards.

Section 4 – Collaborative Problem-Solving

Top-down resolutions may solve immediate issues but can create lingering resentment. Collaborative approaches turn employees into partners in the solution. Involving employees increases buy-in and often surfaces creative solutions supervisors might not have considered.

Steps for collaborative resolution:

- Define the problem together, ensuring agreement on what is being addressed.

- Invite employees to brainstorm potential solutions without judgment.

- Evaluate options for fairness, feasibility, and sustainability.

- Agree on next steps, responsibilities, and review dates.

Collaboration shifts the focus from blame to progress. Employees who help design solutions are more motivated to uphold them.

Section 5 – Managing Emotions in Difficult Conversations

Employee concerns often come with heightened emotions. Supervisors must master their own emotions first to model calm under pressure. When emotions run high, logic alone will not resolve conflict. A supervisor's poise sets the tone.

Strategies for managing emotions:

- Prepare mentally by reviewing facts and potential reactions in advance.

- Maintain calm body language and voice tone even if employees escalate.

- Take a pause or break if conversations become too heated.

- Focus the discussion on behaviors, interests, and solutions rather than personalities.

- Show empathy without surrendering authority or standards.

Grace under pressure is not weakness; it is strength that reassures employees that problems can be resolved fairly.

Section 6 – Following Through on Commitments

Resolution is incomplete without follow-through. Failure to act on commitments destroys credibility and discourages employees from raising issues in the future. Supervisors must ensure that solutions are implemented, monitored, and reinforced.

Follow-through practices include:

- Summarizing agreements in writing and sharing with relevant parties.

- Checking in regularly to evaluate progress and address new concerns.

- Acknowledging improvements and reinforcing positive behaviors.

- Revisiting unresolved issues to ensure closure and avoid recurrence.

Employees measure trustworthiness not by promises made but by promises kept. Consistent follow-through builds loyalty and trust.

Section 7 – Building a Culture of Grace

Grace is not just for crisis moments — it is a culture that supervisors can cultivate daily. A culture of grace balances accountability with empathy, making the workplace a space where employees feel respected and responsible.

Ways to build such a culture:

- Encourage open communication where concerns can be raised early and safely.

- Model humility by admitting mistakes and correcting them openly.

- Provide mediation training or peer support systems for recurring conflicts.

- Recognize employees who contribute constructively to problem-solving.

When grace is woven into culture, challenges become chances to grow rather than reasons to divide.

Public Sector Case Snapshot

At a county health department, employees voiced concerns about uneven scheduling. Some staff felt overburdened while others had lighter workloads. The supervisor responded by analyzing schedule data, holding group discussions, and involving employees in redesigning shifts. The result was greater transparency, more balanced workloads, and improved morale. The supervisor's commitment to fairness and collaboration turned a grievance into an opportunity for improvement.

This case shows that even routine concerns can escalate if ignored, but when addressed with grace, they build stronger teams and cultures.

Applied Tool – The GRACE Framework for Resolution

Use the GRACE framework to resolve concerns with dignity:

G – Gather

- Listen actively, take notes, and collect all relevant facts and perspectives.

R – Respond

- Acknowledge the concern and validate emotions before moving to solutions.

A – Assess

- Investigate facts, identify root causes, and separate issues from personalities.

C – Collaborate

- Work with employees to generate solutions, agreements, and timelines.

E – Execute

- Follow through, monitor progress, and close the loop visibly with employees.

Reflection Questions

15. Do I treat employee concerns as distractions or opportunities for improvement?

16. How skilled am I at listening with empathy under pressure?

17. What steps do I take to ensure fairness and consistency in my responses?

18. How do I involve employees in developing solutions to concerns?

19. What strategies help me manage my own emotions during tense conversations?

20. How do I document and follow through on agreements?

21. Have I created an environment where employees feel safe raising concerns?

22. What lessons have I learned from past grievances or conflicts?

23. How do I reinforce positive outcomes after concerns are resolved?

24. What can I do to strengthen my credibility as a fair and responsive supervisor?

25. How will I model grace and composure for other leaders in my organization?

26. What preventive steps can I take to reduce the recurrence of common concerns?

Leadership-Centered Summary

Supervisors who resolve challenges with grace transform conflict into growth. By listening carefully, responding fairly, collaborating on solutions, and following through with integrity, they build workplaces where employees trust leadership and engage more fully. Challenges will always arise, but handled with grace, they become opportunities to strengthen relationships and culture.

Grace is not softness; it is disciplined empathy in action. It gives employees confidence that even when issues arise, leadership will respond with fairness, respect, and a commitment to resolution. This balance of compassion and accountability sets the standard for professional supervision.

"Grace in supervision is not the absence of challenge but the presence of fairness, empathy, and follow-through."

— *Dr. Patrick C. Patrong*

14 SAFETY AND WELLNESS
Building a Resilient Workplace

Introduction – The Supervisor's Duty of Care

Safety and wellness are often seen as the responsibility of specialized departments — safety officers, HR, or wellness coordinators. Yet supervisors carry a direct duty of care. Every day, they influence whether employees feel physically safe, emotionally supported, and capable of sustaining their work without burning out. A resilient workplace is built not only by policies but also by the daily choices supervisors make.

Consider a transit supervisor who noticed increased absenteeism among bus drivers after a series of minor accidents. Instead of blaming employees, she organized refresher safety training, rotated routes to reduce fatigue, and partnered with HR to launch stress management workshops. Within months, accident rates dropped, morale improved, and turnover slowed. This example highlights how supervisors serve as frontline guardians of both safety and wellness.

This chapter equips supervisors with strategies to build resilience in their teams by promoting safety, encouraging wellness practices, and fostering an environment where employees thrive. By weaving safety and wellness into daily leadership, supervisors can create workplaces where people are both protected and productive.

Section 1 – Understanding Safety and Wellness in the Workplace

Safety refers to freedom from harm, whether physical, psychological, or organizational. Wellness refers to a state of health, balance, and energy that enables sustained performance. Together, they form the foundation of resilience. A workplace may be compliant with safety regulations yet still unwell if employees are exhausted or disengaged.

Dimensions supervisors should pay attention to include:

- Physical safety – preventing accidents, enforcing procedures, and maintaining safe environments.

- Psychological safety – ensuring employees feel safe to speak up without fear of ridicule or retaliation.

- Workload balance – managing assignments to prevent chronic stress and burnout.

- Health promotion – encouraging habits like movement, hydration, and healthy breaks.

- Support systems – fostering peer support, employee assistance programs, and open communication.

Supervisors influence these dimensions by the culture they create, the expectations they set, and the support they provide.

Section 2 – The Supervisor's Role in Promoting Safety

Supervisors are the first line of enforcement for safety. Their commitment to protocols, inspections, and training signals to employees how seriously safety is taken. When supervisors cut corners, employees notice and follow suit. When supervisors model vigilance, employees rise to the standard.

Key responsibilities include:

- Conducting regular safety briefings and refreshers.

- Inspecting work areas and addressing hazards promptly.

- Enforcing use of protective equipment and safe practices.

- Documenting incidents and following up with corrective measures.

- Recognizing employees who demonstrate safety leadership.

Safety is not simply about avoiding accidents; it is about cultivating a culture where everyone feels responsible for protecting one another.

Section 3 – The Supervisor's Role in Promoting Wellness

Wellness goes beyond gym memberships or occasional wellness days. For employees, wellness is shaped by the supervisor's daily practices around workload, flexibility, and recognition. A supervisor who ignores excessive overtime, dismisses stress signals, or models unhealthy work habits undermines wellness. Conversely, supervisors who normalize balance help employees sustain performance long term.

Wellness practices supervisors can champion:

- Encourage employees to take regular breaks and vacations without stigma.

- Balance workloads to prevent chronic overtime or underutilization.

- Acknowledge stress during peak periods and adjust expectations realistically.

- Provide flexibility when possible to accommodate personal or family needs.

- Model healthy behaviors such as leaving on time, taking breaks, and managing stress openly.

- Promote access to available wellness resources, such as Employee Assistance Programs or mindfulness initiatives.

Supervisors who prioritize wellness send the message that people matter as much as results — and in the long run, that improves results.

Section 4 – Integrating Safety and Wellness into Daily Leadership

Safety and wellness cannot be treated as separate silos. They are interdependent. Fatigue, stress, and burnout directly increase the risk of accidents and errors. Likewise, unsafe conditions create stress and reduce wellness. Supervisors should weave both into the same leadership fabric.

Integration strategies include:

- Include wellness check-ins during safety meetings to address both sides of resilience.

- Use data (absenteeism, incidents, turnover) to identify wellness and safety patterns.

- Encourage peer accountability where team members support each other's safety and well-being.

- Celebrate both safety milestones and wellness initiatives equally.

Integration signals to employees that the organization values them as whole people, not just as workers producing output.

Section 5 – Managing Crises with Resilience

Crises — from natural disasters to pandemics — test the resilience of workplaces. Supervisors are often the link between organizational policies and frontline realities. Their leadership during crises can either steady the team or deepen instability.

Principles for crisis management:

- Communicate frequently, clearly, and compassionately — even when information is incomplete.

- Prioritize safety and well-being over productivity when risks are high.

- Adjust workloads and expectations realistically during emergencies.

- Recognize employees for adaptability and courage shown during crises.

- Debrief after crises to learn lessons and build future resilience.

Supervisors who demonstrate calm, care, and adaptability in crises strengthen both safety culture and trust.

Section 6 – Building a Resilient Culture

Resilience is not built overnight; it is cultivated daily through values, routines, and recognition. Supervisors play a vital role in creating a resilient culture where employees feel supported and capable of weathering challenges.

Cultural practices that promote resilience include:

- Embedding safety and wellness into onboarding and ongoing training.

- Encouraging teams to share wellness practices and stress-reduction strategies.

- Recognizing resilience as much as performance in evaluations and rewards.

- Providing access to resources such as EAPs, counseling, or wellness stipends.

When resilience is cultural, employees respond to challenges with adaptability rather than collapse.

Public Sector Case Snapshot

In a municipal water utility, rising heat-related illnesses among field staff prompted concerns. The supervisor responded by revising schedules to avoid peak heat hours, providing hydration stations, and training staff on recognizing early signs of heat stress. Simultaneously, the supervisor encouraged regular check-ins about stress and workload.

Within three months, heat-related incidents dropped significantly, absenteeism declined, and employees reported greater trust in leadership's care for their well-being. This case illustrates how supervisors who integrate safety and wellness practices build resilience and loyalty, even under difficult working conditions.

Applied Tool – The SAFE-WELL Framework for Supervisors

Use the SAFE-WELL framework to integrate safety and wellness:

- **S – Scan:** Observe the environment and identify hazards or stress points regularly.

- **A – Act:** Address risks or stressors immediately with corrective measures.

- **F – Foster:** Build a culture where employees look out for each other's safety and wellness.

- **E – Educate:** Provide training and resources to strengthen awareness and skills.

- **W – Watch:** Monitor data trends in incidents, absenteeism, and morale.

- **E – Encourage:** Recognize and reward safety and wellness contributions.

- **L – Lead:** Model safe practices and healthy habits consistently.

- **L – Learn:** Debrief incidents and wellness challenges to build continuous improvement.

Reflection Questions

1. How do I define my duty of care as a supervisor for safety and wellness?

2. What daily practices can I adopt to demonstrate commitment to both safety and wellness?

3. How do I integrate wellness check-ins into regular team routines?

4. What hazards or stressors are most pressing for my team?

5. How do I balance productivity with employee well-being?

6. How prepared am I to lead during crises or emergencies?

7. How do I model healthy behaviors that employees can emulate?

8. What resources (EAP, training, health services) can I connect employees to more consistently?

9. How do I ensure safety and wellness are recognized equally with performance?

10. How do I create a culture where employees look out for each other's safety and well-being?

11. What lessons have I learned from past safety or wellness challenges that I can apply now?

Leadership-Centered Summary

Supervisors are frontline architects of resilient workplaces. By embedding safety and wellness into daily leadership, they protect employees from harm, prevent burnout, and promote long-term performance. The most successful supervisors do not view safety and wellness as competing with productivity but as enabling it. Healthy, supported employees are more focused, loyal, and innovative.

As you lead, remember that resilience is built in ordinary days as much as in crises. Every safety check, every wellness conversation, and every demonstration of care adds up to a culture where employees thrive. Supervisors who champion resilience leave a legacy of teams that are not only effective but sustainable.

"Resilient workplaces are built when supervisors champion both safety and wellness every day."

— *Dr. Patrick C. Patrong*

15 THE FINANCIAL CONDUCTOR
Supervisors and the Budget Maestro

Introduction – Supervisors as Stewards of Resources

Supervisors are often thought of as people-managers, but they are also resource stewards. Every decision they make — scheduling overtime, approving supply orders, or assigning equipment — has financial implications. Even if supervisors are not accountants, they function as budget conductors, orchestrating resources in a way that supports mission success. A financially aware supervisor protects both the team and the organization from waste, inefficiency, and reputational risk.

Consider a public library supervisor who noticed ballooning overtime costs due to last-minute scheduling gaps. By tracking patterns, cross-training staff, and adjusting schedules proactively, the supervisor reduced overtime by 40% while maintaining service levels. The savings funded new technology for patrons. This story illustrates how supervisors act as financial conductors, directing limited resources toward maximum impact.

This chapter offers supervisors practical guidance for managing budgets at their level of responsibility. We will explore the basics of financial stewardship, cost control, forecasting, and accountability. Tools and examples will help you balance mission needs with fiscal responsibility.

Section 1 – Understanding the Supervisor's Financial Role

Supervisors are rarely responsible for drafting organizational budgets, but they are critical to execution. Their decisions influence whether budget plans succeed or fail. Understanding the supervisor's financial role begins with recognizing that every dollar is connected to outcomes, and waste in one area limits capacity in another.

Supervisor's financial responsibilities include:

- Monitoring daily expenses like supplies, overtime, and equipment use.
- Tracking budget lines relevant to their unit or department.
- Ensuring compliance with procurement policies.
- Providing input for budget forecasts and adjustments.
- Communicating financial realities to their teams.

Financial stewardship is not about micromanaging pennies; it is about aligning spending with purpose and demonstrating accountability.

Section 2 – Building Financial Awareness

Supervisors must develop financial literacy to make informed decisions. This does not require advanced accounting knowledge but does require awareness of terms, reports, and trends.

Steps to build financial awareness:

- Learn the budget categories and codes relevant to your team.
- Review monthly or quarterly budget reports and ask questions.
- Track spending patterns in your area (supplies, overtime, training).
- Understand cost drivers such as seasonal demand or staff turnover.
- Engage with finance staff or mentors to strengthen understanding.

Financial awareness builds credibility. Teams trust supervisors who can explain the 'why' behind spending decisions.

Section 3 – Cost Control Without Cutting Corners

Supervisors face pressure to control costs, but savings must not come at the expense of safety, quality, or morale. Effective cost control identifies efficiencies rather than imposing arbitrary cuts.

Strategies for responsible cost control:

- Analyze overtime trends and address root causes through staffing plans.

- Encourage conservation of supplies and monitor trends.

- Cross-train employees to reduce reliance on overtime or temporary staff.

- Leverage technology for efficiency in scheduling, reporting, or communication.

- Negotiate vendor terms within procurement guidelines.

Cost control should be communicated as stewardship, not deprivation. Employees are more willing to support savings when they see reinvestment in mission priorities.

Section 4 – Forecasting and Planning

Budget execution is not static. Supervisors must anticipate changes in demand, workload, and costs. Forecasting helps prevent surprises and ensures readiness for opportunities or emergencies.

Forecasting practices include:

- Review past spending patterns to predict future needs.

- Identify cyclical costs such as seasonal staffing or utility spikes.

- Anticipate risks such as equipment failure or policy changes.

- Submit budget adjustment requests early when trends emerge.

- Use simple spreadsheets or tools to track and project spending.

Planning demonstrates leadership. A supervisor who anticipates needs shows foresight and earns trust from leadership.

Section 5 – Communicating About Finances

Transparency about financial realities builds trust. Supervisors should explain budget constraints and involve employees in cost-conscious practices.

Communication strategies include:

- Share relevant budget updates at team meetings to build awareness.

- Explain the 'why' behind restrictions or cost-saving measures.

- Celebrate savings that fund reinvestments in the team.

- Invite employee suggestions for efficiency and recognize contributions.

Employees respond better to constraints when they understand the bigger picture. Communication turns financial discipline into a shared responsibility.

Section 6 – Accountability and Ethics in Financial Stewardship

Supervisors are accountable not only for results but also for integrity in financial practices. Misuse of funds, even unintentionally, damages credibility and can have serious consequences.

Accountability practices include:

- Adhere strictly to procurement and approval processes.

- Avoid conflicts of interest or appearances of favoritism in spending.

- Maintain accurate, timely records of financial transactions.

- Encourage a culture where employees report potential financial concerns.

Ethical stewardship ensures that resources serve the mission and protect the public trust.

Public Sector Case Snapshot

In a state transportation office, rising overtime costs threatened project budgets. A supervisor conducted a three-month analysis, identifying that unplanned absences created cascading coverage issues. She introduced staggered schedules and cross-trained staff to cover specialized tasks. Overtime decreased by 35%, and employee fatigue declined. The savings funded safety upgrades across worksites. Her proactive financial stewardship reinforced accountability and improved both morale and service delivery.

Applied Tool – The BUDGET Framework for Supervisors

Use the BUDGET framework to manage finances responsibly:

- **B – Balance:** Balance mission needs with financial limits.

- **U – Understand:** Learn codes, reports, and cost drivers relevant to your unit.

- **D – Document:** Keep accurate records of expenses and savings.

- **G – Guide:** Lead employees in cost-conscious behaviors and practices.

- **E – Evaluate:** Review spending patterns regularly and adjust as needed.

- **T – Transparently Communicate:** Share financial realities and celebrate smart stewardship.

Reflection Questions

1. How do my daily supervisory decisions impact financial outcomes?

2. What budget categories or cost drivers am I least familiar with, and how can I learn more?

3. Where can efficiencies be gained without reducing safety, quality, or morale?

4. What forecasting practices can I adopt to anticipate future needs?

5. How do I communicate financial realities to my team in a transparent way?

6. How do I model financial stewardship for my employees?

7. What accountability measures do I use to prevent misuse of funds?

8. How can I strengthen partnerships with finance staff to improve decision-making?

9. What ethical dilemmas might arise in financial stewardship, and how would I respond?

10. How will I measure my effectiveness as a financial conductor?

Leadership-Centered Summary

Supervisors are conductors of financial stewardship, orchestrating limited resources in ways that advance mission and protect public trust. By building financial awareness, controlling costs responsibly, forecasting needs, and communicating transparently, supervisors demonstrate leadership that extends beyond people management. Financially responsible supervisors earn credibility with both employees and executives by showing that they can balance compassion with accountability, and resources with results.

When supervisors embrace their role as financial conductors, they not only preserve budgets but also elevate the effectiveness and resilience of their teams.

"Financial stewardship is not about cutting costs — it is about conducting resources with wisdom and integrity."

— Dr. Patrick C. Patrong

16: EXCEPTIONAL SERVICE, EXCEPTIONAL SUPERVISORS

Introduction – Service as Leadership

Exceptional supervisors understand that leadership is service. Their role is not only to manage tasks but also to model how service excellence drives team reputation, customer satisfaction, and organizational trust. Whether the 'customer' is an external client, a citizen, or an internal colleague, supervisors set the tone. Service quality, good or bad, is amplified under their leadership.

Consider a motor vehicle department supervisor whose office was notorious for long waits and frustrated patrons. Instead of blaming staff or dismissing complaints, she studied the service process, held listening sessions with employees, and piloted a ticketing system to streamline flow. She also empowered clerks to resolve minor issues without escalation. Within six months, wait times dropped by half and satisfaction scores soared. Her leadership demonstrated how supervisors transform service culture.

This chapter explores how supervisors can create exceptional service environments by setting expectations, empowering employees, responding to feedback, and modeling professionalism. It provides tools for integrating service excellence into daily supervision, even in challenging public sector contexts.

Section 1 – Defining Service Excellence in the Public Sector

Service excellence is not perfection. It is consistent, reliable, and respectful service that meets or exceeds expectations. For supervisors, it requires balancing efficiency with empathy.

Core principles of service excellence include:

- Consistency – delivering the same standard every time.

- Clarity – providing accurate information and instructions.

- Empathy – acknowledging the customer's experience and emotions.

- Responsiveness – addressing issues promptly and constructively.

- Accountability – owning mistakes and making corrections visible.

Supervisors who champion these principles teach their teams that service is not an afterthought but the essence of credibility.

Section 2 – The Supervisor's Role in Service Quality

Supervisors directly influence how employees deliver service. From coaching communication to modeling patience under pressure, supervisors shape culture. When supervisors tolerate rudeness, lateness, or indifference, employees learn that service quality is optional. When they recognize and reinforce excellence, employees prioritize it.

Supervisor responsibilities for service quality include:

- Set clear service standards and explain their importance.

- Observe service interactions and provide constructive feedback.

- Recognize employees who demonstrate service excellence.

- Intervene promptly when service falls below standard.

- Model patience, professionalism, and respectful interactions.

Supervisors act as service role models. Their tone, language, and attitude toward customers become the unspoken script employees follow.

Section 3 – Empowering Employees to Deliver Exceptional Service

Exceptional service depends on employee empowerment. Supervisors who micromanage decisions delay service and frustrate customers. Empowered employees resolve issues quickly, confidently, and creatively.

Ways supervisors can empower employees:

- Delegate authority to handle routine service issues without supervisor approval.

- Provide training in problem-solving and customer communication.

- Equip employees with tools and resources to meet customer needs.

- Encourage innovation by recognizing creative service solutions.

- Support employees publicly when they make reasonable service decisions.

Empowered employees not only improve service quality but also feel more engaged and respected.

Section 4 – Listening to Customers and Employees

Service excellence requires continuous feedback. Supervisors must listen to both customers and employees to identify patterns and opportunities.

Feedback practices include:

- Collect customer feedback through surveys, suggestion boxes, or digital platforms.

- Hold team debriefs after peak periods to reflect on service strengths and gaps.

- Invite employees to share insights from front-line interactions.

- Respond visibly to feedback by making changes and communicating outcomes.

Listening demonstrates respect for voices inside and outside the organization. Ignoring feedback, on the other hand, signals indifference and erodes trust.

Section 5 – Handling Service Breakdowns Gracefully

Service failures are inevitable. Systems crash, supplies run out, or employees make mistakes. What distinguishes exceptional supervisors is how they respond.

Principles for handling service breakdowns:

- Acknowledge the failure quickly and sincerely.

- Apologize without defensiveness and explain the cause transparently.

- Provide an immediate alternative or workaround when possible.

- Communicate updates clearly so customers and employees know progress is being made.

- Follow up to ensure resolution and satisfaction.

- Debrief with the team to prevent recurrence.

Handled well, a service failure can actually strengthen trust. Customers and employees remember when leaders took ownership and corrected problems with grace.

Section 6 – Building a Service-Oriented Culture

A culture of service excellence emerges when supervisors reinforce it daily. Service becomes embedded in hiring, training, recognition, and evaluation.

Steps to build culture:

- Integrate service values into onboarding and orientation.

- Include service excellence as a criterion in performance evaluations.

- Celebrate stories of outstanding service in meetings or newsletters.

- Link service success to organizational mission and community impact.

- Encourage peer recognition of service excellence.

Culture is sustained not by posters or slogans but by the behaviors supervisors recognize and reward every day.

Public Sector Case Snapshot

At a city permit office, long lines and frustrated citizens had become the norm. A new supervisor implemented a triage system at the entrance, directed simple requests to a quick-service window, and empowered clerks to approve minor variances without managerial sign-off. She also recognized employees who handled tense interactions with professionalism. Within months, wait times decreased significantly and public trust improved. The supervisor's actions demonstrated how leadership shapes service culture.

Applied Tool – The SERVE Framework for Supervisors

Use the SERVE framework to deliver exceptional service:

- **S – Set Standards:** Define clear, measurable service expectations for your team.

- **E – Empower Employees:** Give staff authority and resources to resolve issues quickly.

- **R – Recognize Excellence:** Celebrate employees who model outstanding service behaviors.

- **V – Value Feedback:** Seek and act on input from customers and employees.

- **E – Elevate Culture:** Integrate service excellence into daily routines and recognition.

Reflection Questions

1. How do I define exceptional service in my supervisory context?

2. What service standards have I communicated clearly to my team?

3. How do I model service excellence in my interactions with employees and customers?

4. What authority or tools can I delegate to empower employees for faster service?

5. How do I encourage creativity and innovation in solving service problems?

6. What feedback mechanisms do I use to capture customer and employee experiences?

7. How do I respond to service breakdowns to preserve trust and credibility?

8. What recognition practices do I use to reinforce service excellence?

9. How do I connect service excellence to our mission and community impact?

10. What cultural practices in my team reinforce or undermine service values?

11. What service stories can I share to inspire my team?

12. How will I measure the impact of improved service on organizational outcomes?

Leadership-Centered Summary

Service excellence is leadership in action. Supervisors who define clear standards, empower employees, listen actively, and handle breakdowns with grace create workplaces where exceptional service is the norm. They understand that service quality defines reputation, trust, and mission success.

By embedding service into culture and modeling it daily, supervisors transform both employee experience and customer outcomes. Exceptional supervisors do not just manage service — they elevate it.

"Exceptional supervisors know that service excellence is not a task, but a culture they build every day."

— Dr. Patrick C. Patrong

17 THE SUPERVISOR'S LEGACY
Leaving a Mark of Excellence

Introduction – Beyond the Present Moment

Supervisors often focus on immediate results: meeting deadlines, resolving conflicts, and keeping operations running smoothly. Yet the true measure of supervisory success lies in the legacy they leave. A legacy is not defined by titles or projects but by the culture, people, and practices that remain after a supervisor moves on. Every decision, conversation, and example contributes to this legacy — either building trust and growth or leaving gaps and resentment.

Think of a school administrator who retired after twenty years. Former staff recalled her fairness, mentorship, and dedication to student success. Her influence continued through the teachers she trained, the policies she shaped, and the values she instilled. Her legacy lived on in the daily practices of the institution. This illustrates the essence of supervisory legacy: it is carried forward by others long after the supervisor has departed.

This chapter examines how supervisors can intentionally craft a legacy of excellence. We will explore the dimensions of personal values, team development, organizational culture, and mentorship. Practical tools and reflective questions will help you align daily actions with the lasting impact you want to leave.

Section 1 – Defining Legacy in Supervision

Legacy in supervision is the cumulative effect of a supervisor's leadership on people, processes, and culture. Unlike short-term achievements, legacy reflects what endures after the supervisor leaves.

Key dimensions of legacy include:

- **People** – the skills, confidence, and team members' growth
- **Processes** – the systems and practices that continue to guide work.
- **Culture** – the values and norms embedded daily.
- **Reputation** – the credibility and trust the supervisor establishes with colleagues and stakeholders.

A supervisor's legacy is not accidental; intentional leadership choices shape it.

Section 2 – Values as the Foundation of Legacy

Values are the anchor of legacy. They guide decisions and shape the environment supervisors create. Supervisors who consistently demonstrate integrity, fairness, and respect leave behind cultures where those values endure.

Practical ways supervisors reinforce values:

- Make decisions transparently, explaining the rationale to employees.
- Demonstrate fairness in assigning opportunities and responsibilities.
- Model respect in every interaction, regardless of role/status.
- Hold yourself accountable for mistakes and corrections.

Values-driven leadership ensures that what lasts is not only efficiency but also ethical standards and trust.

Section 3 – Developing People as Legacy

The most enduring legacy a supervisor leaves is the growth of people. Skills and systems may fade, but empowered employees carry forward what they learned. Supervisors should see every coaching conversation, every delegation, and every recognition as an investment in legacy.

Strategies to build people-focused legacy:

- Mentor emerging leaders within your team.

- Encourage professional development and support training opportunities.

- Delegate stretch assignments that prepare employees for future roles.

- Celebrate growth, not just results, in performance evaluations.

Supervisors who prioritize people development multiply their influence far beyond their tenure.

Section 4 – Embedding Culture as Legacy

Culture is the unwritten code of behavior in a workplace. Supervisors directly shape culture by what they tolerate, encourage, and reward. A culture of accountability, respect, and service outlasts individual supervisors when it becomes the norm.

Steps to embed culture:

- Align team practices with organizational mission and values.

- Reinforce desired behaviors through recognition.

- Address negative behaviors to prevent cultural erosion.

- Create rituals or traditions that reinforce positive identity.

Culture is not what a supervisor says; it is what the team learns to expect daily.

Section 5 – Mentorship and Legacy

Mentorship extends legacy beyond immediate teams. Supervisors who mentor peers or leaders in other units influence the broader organization. Mentorship also ensures that knowledge and wisdom are passed forward rather than lost.

Mentorship practices include:

- Offer guidance to colleagues new to leadership roles.
- Share lessons learned from mistakes as well as successes.
- Encourage cross-team collaboration and sharing.
- Stay accessible as a sounding board.

Mentorship transforms legacy from personal achievement to institutional strength.

Public Sector Case Snapshot

In a state health agency, a supervisor was promoted after ten years. Colleagues noted that his legacy was visible in the new supervisors he had coached. They led with fairness, communicated transparently, and modeled accountability just as he had. His influence had created a ripple effect, shaping leadership across the organization. This case demonstrates how legacy multiplies when supervisors invest in people and culture.

Applied Tool – The LEGACY Framework for Supervisors

Use the LEGACY framework to craft a positive mark:

- **L – Lead with Values:** Demonstrate integrity, fairness, and respect daily.
- **E – Empower People:** Develop employees through mentoring, delegation, and recognition.

- **G – Grow Culture:** Reinforce accountability, service, and respect as cultural norms.

- **A – Align Practices:** Ensure decisions and routines reflect organizational mission.

- **C – Communicate Continuity:** Share knowledge and processes to outlast your tenure.

- **Y – Yield Influence:** Recognize that legacy is measured not by control but by lasting impact.

Reflection Questions

1. What do I want my legacy as a supervisor to be remembered for?

2. How do my daily actions reflect my values and leadership philosophy?

3. What growth opportunities am I creating for my team members?

4. How do I embed positive cultural practices into daily routines?

5. Who am I mentoring, and how will they carry forward my influence?

6. What systems or processes have I strengthened that will endure beyond me?

7. How am I modeling accountability in ways that others can emulate?

8. What stories will colleagues tell about my leadership when I move on?

9. What negative patterns do I need to address now to avoid leaving a harmful legacy?

10. How do I balance immediate results with long-term impact?

11. What traditions can I establish to reinforce team identity?

12. How will I measure whether I am building the legacy I intend?

Leadership-Centered Summary

Supervisory legacy is not left to chance. It is shaped intentionally by values, people, culture, and mentorship. Every decision contributes to the story others will tell about your leadership. By focusing on fairness, development, accountability, and service, supervisors create legacies that strengthen both people and institutions.

A supervisor's true success is measured not by the span of their authority but by the endurance of their influence. When supervisors leave behind stronger people, resilient cultures, and enduring values, they have left a mark of excellence.

"Legacy is the echo of leadership — it continues to shape people and culture long after the supervisor has moved on."

— Dr. Patrick C. Patrong

18 Conclusion

Final Reflections on Supervisory Success

Introduction – The Journey Completed, the Work Continues

Supervisory success is not a single destination but an ongoing journey. Each chapter in this book has equipped you with strategies, tools, and reflections to help you lead with clarity, courage, and compassion. As you bring these lessons together, remember that supervision is more than managing processes or enforcing rules — it is about shaping people, culture, and futures. This concluding chapter reinforces the lessons learned, highlights key takeaways, and offers an inspirational call to action for every supervisor.

The supervisors who leave the greatest impact are those who see themselves as stewards of both people and purpose. Their influence extends beyond the present moment, building a legacy that continues long after they move on. This chapter encourages you to view your role through that lens of stewardship and long-term influence.

Section 1 – The Core Lessons of Supervisory Success

Across the book, several core lessons have emerged. These lessons form the bedrock of successful supervision. While each chapter explored them in detail, here they are reinforced as guiding pillars:

- Supervision is about people first — tasks and processes matter, but people drive results.

- Clarity of expectations builds trust and reduces conflict.

- Consistency and fairness establish credibility and loyalty.

- Communication, both active listening and clear direction, is a supervisor's most powerful tool.

- Accountability should be developmental, not punitive.

- Empowered of employees multiplies capacity and engagement.

- Recognition fuels motivation and strengthens culture.

These are not one-time actions but continuous practices. Supervisory excellence is measured by how consistently these lessons are applied.

Section 2 – Embracing the Supervisor's Dual Identity

Supervisors walk a fine line between management and leadership. They must enforce rules while also inspiring vision. This dual identity is not a contradiction but a complement. Effective supervisors learn to navigate the tension between holding people accountable and encouraging them to grow.

Practical applications of dual identity include:

- Balancing discipline with coaching, ensuring that accountability leads to growth.

- Using authority wisely, not to dominate but to protect fairness and mission integrity.

- Adapting communication styles to both organizational leaders above and employees below.

Supervisors who master this dual identity earn respect across all levels of the organization.

Section 3 – Building a Sustainable Culture of Success

Culture outlasts supervisors. A healthy, productive culture ensures that excellence continues regardless of leadership transitions. Supervisors play a vital role in embedding values and practices that become self-sustaining.

Key cultural contributions of supervisors include:

- Normalizing accountability as a positive and shared responsibility.

- Embedding recognition into daily practices rather than occasional gestures.

- Creating an environment of psychological safety where ideas and concerns are voiced openly.

- Linking individual tasks to broader organizational mission and purpose.

When supervisors focus on building culture, they move from temporary managers to enduring leaders.

Section 4 – Preparing for Future Challenges

The supervisory landscape is constantly evolving. Technology, workforce demographics, economic pressures, and public expectations reshape the context in which supervisors operate. Success requires adaptability and a commitment to lifelong learning.

Supervisors can prepare by:

- Staying informed about trends in leadership, management, and technology.

- Engaging in professional development opportunities and encouraging employees to do the same.

- Building networks of peers and mentors for support and shared learning.

- Reflecting regularly on personal growth and adjusting leadership style accordingly.

Supervisors who anticipate change and embrace growth lead with confidence, even in uncertain times.

Section 5 – A Call to Supervisory Excellence

At the heart of supervision lies responsibility: responsibility for people, for results, and for culture. This book has given you tools and reflections, but the real transformation will happen in your daily practice. The call to supervisory excellence is not about perfection; it is about persistence — showing up consistently with integrity, empathy, and courage.

As you continue your journey, remember:

- Every decision shapes your legacy.

- Every interaction influences culture.

- Every challenge is an opportunity to demonstrate grace and resilience.

- Every success is multiplied when shared with the team.

Your mark as a supervisor is not written in reports or metrics alone but in the lives you influence and the culture you create.

Section 6 – Key Takeaways Summary for Supervisors

To provide a quick-reference guide, here are the key takeaways from across the chapters, condensed into actionable insights:

- Lead with values: Integrity, fairness, and respect are non-negotiables.

- Communicate with clarity and listen with empathy.

- Set expectations early and reinforce them consistently.

- Balance accountability with development and support.

- Recognize contributions in ways that matter to individuals.

- Build culture intentionally; do not leave it to chance.

- Model resilience in times of crisis and uncertainty.

- Mentor others to multiply leadership capacity.

This summary can serve as a desk reference — a reminder that supervisory excellence is both art and science, requiring both practical skills and principled character.

Leadership-Centered Summary

Supervisory success is a lifelong journey of growth, reflection, and service. You now have a toolbox of strategies and frameworks to guide you, but your greatest asset will be the character and consistency you bring to the role. As you lead teams, remember that your influence extends far beyond the present moment. Your words and actions shape legacies, empower futures, and define cultures.

Carry forward the lessons of this book not as static rules but as living practices. Apply them with wisdom, adapt them to context, and embody them with authenticity. In doing so, you will leave a mark of excellence — a legacy of leadership that will inspire others long after your supervisory role has ended.

"Supervisory success is not about the position you hold, but the lives you shape and the culture you leave behind."

— Dr. Patrick C. Patrong

ABOUT THE AUTHOR

Dr. Patrick C. Patrong is an accomplished leader, consultant, and speaker with over 30 years of experience transforming organizations through people-centered leadership. He currently serves as Assistant Deputy Director at the Virginia Museum of Fine Arts and is President of Patrong Enterprises Inc., a firm dedicated to leadership development, organizational growth, and employee empowerment.

A graduate of multiple executive leadership academies and a certified Lean Six Sigma Black Belt, Dr. Patrong holds a Doctorate in Strategic Leadership. His philosophy centers on creating opportunity-driven cultures where supervisors are equipped to inspire growth, build trust, and lead with integrity.

Known for his engaging "Magic with a Message" teaching style, Dr. Patrong blends practical insight with memorable storytelling and interactive demonstrations. His work spans public sector agencies, universities, and cultural institutions, where he has guided leaders through change, coached teams toward resilience, and developed innovative leadership programs such as the Supervisory Learning Experience (SLE) and the PAAL™ system (Posture, Attire, Attitude, and Language).

Beyond his professional achievements, Dr. Patrong is a photographer, mentor, and creative entrepreneur who integrates his cultural heritage and artistic vision into his leadership approach. His lifelong commitment is summed up in the guiding principle of his firm: "Transforming Organizations – One Employee at a Time."

www.ingramcontent.com/pod-product-compliance
Lightning Source LLC
Chambersburg PA
CBHW072352090426
42741CB00012B/3021